Modeling the Dream CD

Dream CD
Walkthroughs and Flybys II

by Phil Shatz

Waite Group Press™
Corte Madera, CA

PUBLISHER Mitchell Waite
EDITOR-IN-CHIEF Scott Calamar
EDITORIAL DIRECTOR Joel Fugazzotto
MANAGING EDITOR Joe Ferrie
CONTENT EDITOR Ann Krueger Spivak
TECHNICAL COORDINATOR David Middleton
PRODUCTION DIRECTOR Julianne Ososke
DESIGNER/PROJECT COORDINATOR Sestina Quarequio
COPY EDITOR Marianne Krcma
PRODUCTION Marlyn Amann
ILLUSTRATIONS Pat Rogondino
COVER DESIGN Michael Rogondino

© 1994 by The Waite Group, Inc.®
Published by Waite Group Press™, 200 Tamal Plaza, Corte Madera, CA 94925.

Waite Group Press™ is distributed to bookstores and book wholesalers by Publishers Group West, Box 8843, Emeryville, CA 94662, 1-800-638-9369.

Printed in the United States of America
94 95 96 97 • 10 9 8 7 6 5 4 3 2 1

Library of Congress Cataloging-in-Publication Data
Shatz, Phil
    Modeling the dream CD walkthroughs and flybys II / by Phil Shatz.
        p. cm.
    Continues : Walkthroughs and flybys CD
    Includes index.
    ISBN: 1-878739-67-0 : $32.95
    1. Computer animation. 2. Three-dimensional display systems. 3. Computer sound processing.
I. Shatz, Phil. Walkthroughs and flybys CD.   II. Title.
TR897.7.S53 1994
006.6--dc20
                                                            94-20915
                                                               CIP

Dedication

For my clients, especially Waite Group Press.
Thanks for having the faith in me to deliver what I've promised.

About the Author
and Principal Contributors

While the vast majority of this work was put together by Phil, two others made such significant contributions that there is no way the book could have been written without them. Without Rob Wallace's music and sound effects or Simon Browne's SpaceBar this product would be woefully lacking as a guide to state-of-the-art multimedia development.

Phil Shatz

Phil got his start with PCs while working on a political science degree at Syracuse University. His only application of computing to politics was an internship spent as director of data processing for an unsuccessful mayoral campaign. While it was fun earning academic credit for trying to take city hall, he decided that politics was just too messy to seriously pursue. His first job was as technical support manager for Show Partner, an onscreen presentation package. Upon leaving that position in 1988, Phil produced demos for Lotus, Computer Associates, Adobe Systems, and Intel.

After moving to the UK in 1990, Phil did a three-year stint as technical director of Screen Artists Ltd., a PC graphics service bureau and consultancy. Besides producing graphics for press conferences, training seminars, and demo disks, at Screen Artists Phil compiled a CD-ROM-based collection of PC graphics called DANGER! Hot Stuff. Currently Phil runs Media Development Services, a CD development house and multimedia service bureau near London's Victoria Station. He can be reached on the Internet at 76470.233@compuserve.com.

Rob Wallace

Rob lives in Glendale, a suburb of Phoenix, Arizona, with his wife Jean and her two sons, Bobby and David Gill. His MIDI and digital sound studio is located in his home along with the office for Wallace Music and Sound, Inc. Rob has produced music and sound effects for dozens of computer games and educational products, as well as a musical score for a motion picture and music for television and radio commercials. Rob's performance credits also include voice characterizations for digital soundtracks.

Multimedia Kaleidosonics, from Masque Publishing, is Rob's most recent software release. It comes complete with a 48-minute audio soundtrack featuring 15 original songs by Rob produced at Wallace Music. A shortened bannerware version of Kaleidosonics can be found on the enclosed CD.

The dozens of products Rob has worked on include: The Miracle Piano Teaching System (The Software Toolworks), Mig 29 (Spectrum Holobyte), Monster Bash and Hocus Pocus (Apogee), Mario's Missing Deluxe and World Atlas (The Software Toolworks), as well as Sea Wolf and Eagle Eye Mysteries (Electronic Arts).

Rob can be reached on the Internet at 29220@ef.gc.maricopa.edu.

Simon Browne

Simon started working with computers in an ink factory back in 1987. Armed with the then-popular BBC Micro, he developed experimental systems to drive equipment on the shop floor. Simon's strong mathematical background led him to focus a great deal of his energy on creating mathematical models to simulate process conditions. Soon he moved up to running AutoCAD on an Apricot 286. Although the 3D capabilities of that version of AutoCAD were negligible, he put them to good use in the design of new machinery. As AutoCAD advanced through the years, Simon focused on its programmable aspects and became proficient in the AutoLISP language.

With the release of Autodesk 3D Studio, Simon decided to take the leap and start up his own business producing visualizations and conducting training seminars. At present he runs a service bureau equipped with five 486 and Pentium machines that constantly churn out graphics for rock videos, corporate advertisements, and even furniture design.

Simon can be reached on the Internet at 100410,534@compuserve.com.

Table of Contents

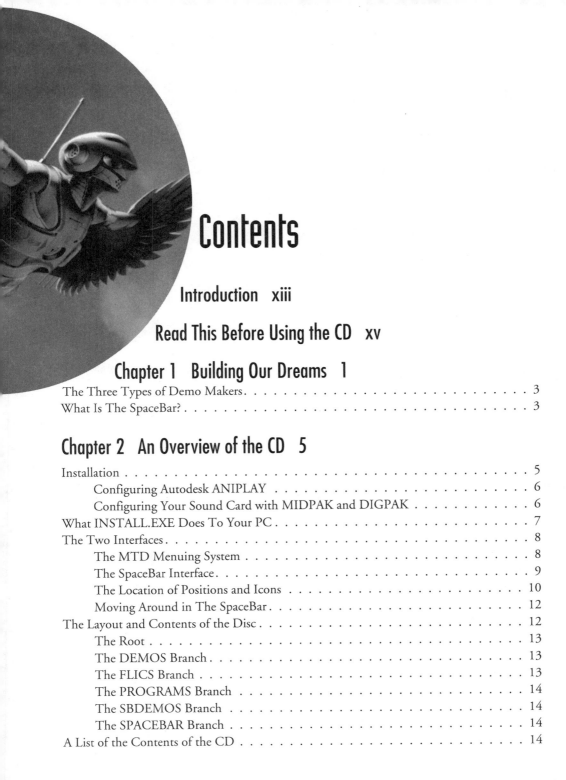

Contents

Chapter 5 3D Animations 53

Chapter 6   Sound Blaster Demos   77

Chapter 7   General Demonstrations   97

Appendix A   Contributor Listings   109

Appendix B   Troubleshooting   113

Appendix C   Sources   117

Index   125

Acknowledgments

The following people and organizations, all of whom I am glad to have this opportunity to heartily thank, were a tremendous help in the creation of this book.

First, to my editor, Joe Ferrie, for his support throughout the ups and downs of this project. There is nothing like his positive and reassuring "voice" always there at the other end of the net. Next comes Karin Smyth for coordinating the many contributor mailings and generally keeping everything on track while we were planning the project and acquiring data. Simon Browne did an excellent job with The SpaceBar 3D modeling and his thorough guide to using 3D Studio which constitutes Chapter 4. Our other main collaborator, Rob Wallace, wrote some excellent tunes and created dozens of brilliant sound effects in addition to delivering a great chapter about composing for PC games and multimedia. Without Jason Gibbs' endless support, advice, and programming skills, we would have been totally stuck on a number of occasions. His adaptation of John Ratcliff's MIDPAK and DIGPAK into a Grasp extension were a major breakthrough. Otto Chrons' DMP music player combined with music from The Future Crew took our "BigDemo" to a new level.

Also, thanks to Ann Spivak for a tremendous content edit, Ed Suthon at Pitman Publishing for putting up with my hair-brained marketing schemes, and Thorsten von Vietinghoff at CeQuadrat for the copy of WinOnCD premastering software. Thanks to John Smith at Advanced Gravis for the Gravis UltraSound card, Paul Fletcher at Creative Labs UK for too many things to even begin to mention, and finally to my friends Ulrik Henriksen and Samuli Syvahuoko for keeping me in touch with The Scene. Greetings to the following groups: BrainBug, Cascada, DarkZone, Epical, Future Crew, Iguana, Sonic, Silents, Surprise!, Triton, Witan, and Xography.

Dear Reader:

What is a book? Is it perpetually fated to be inky words on a paper page? Or can a book simply be something that inspires—feeding your head with ideas and creativity regardless of the medium? The latter, I believe. That's why I'm always pushing our books to a higher plane; using new technology to reinvent the medium.

I wrote my first book in 1973, *Projects in Sights, Sounds, and Sensations*. I like to think of it as our first multimedia book. In the years since then, I've learned that people want to *experience* information, not just passively absorb it—they want interactive MTV in a book. With this in mind, I started my own publishing company and published *Master C*, a book/disk package that turned the PC into a C language instructor. Then we branched out to computer graphics with *Fractal Creations*, which included a color poster, 3D glasses, and a totally rad fractal generator. Ever since, we've included disks and other goodies with most of our books. *Virtual Reality Creations* is bundled with 3D Fresnel viewing goggles and *Walkthroughs and Flybys CD* comes with a multimedia CD-ROM. We've made complex multimedia accessible for any PC user with *Ray Tracing Creations, Multimedia Creations, Making Movies on Your PC, Image Lab,* and three books on Fractals.

The Waite Group continues to publish innovative multimedia books on cutting-edge topics, and of course the programming books that make up our heritage. Being a programmer myself, I appreciate clear guidance through a tricky OS, so our books come bundled with disks and CDs loaded with code, utilities, and custom controls.

By 1994, The Waite Group will have published 135 books. Our next step is to develop a new type of book, an interactive, multimedia experience involving the reader on many levels.

With this new book, you'll be trained by a computer-based instructor with infinite patience, run a simulation to visualize the topic, play a game that shows you different aspects of the subject, interact with others on-line, and have instant access to a large database on the subject. For traditionalists, there will be a full-color, paper-based book.

In the meantime, they've wired the White House for hi-tech; the information super-highway has been proposed; and computers, communication, entertainment, and information are becoming inseparable. To travel in this Digital Age you'll need guidebooks. The Waite Group offers such guidance for the most important software—your mind.

We hope you enjoy this book. For a color catalog, just fill out and send in the Reader Report Card at the back of the book.

Sincerely,

Mitchell Waite

Mitchell Waite
Publisher

Waite
Group
Press™

Introduction

Walkthroughs and Flybys CD was quite successful, but it didn't tell enough of the story. As a collection of short tales about multimedia development projects, it has helped over 50,000 readers in four languages gain some insight into the nuts and bolts of being a new-media, digital artist. The short stories approach, however, didn't contain enough hands-on information to satisfy some of our readers. That's why we've taken a much more technical focus in this book.

   Modeling the Dream CD teaches you what it takes to compose music and sound effects for synchronization with 3D animation. It provides a detailed description of how to design a 3D world with Autodesk 3D Studio, the "Black and Decker" of virtual reality. In addition, the underlying code structure that holds everything together has been left as open, unencrypted Grasp source code. Our explanations of this code will help you understand how interactive multimedia really works. And to help you raise your sights, we present the work of over 40 new artists and describe their work in much the same manner as we did in the first book.

Why We Wrote This Book

Perhaps the biggest reason we decided to write this book has been the resounding clamor for more. The tone of readers' comments in email messages, faxes, and general inquiries clearly pointed out that there is considerable demand for quality demos as long as they are presented in an organized fashion that provides some insight into how they were made. Our hope is that you find the insights you are looking for and thoroughly enjoy what you will see.

   We almost called this book "You Like to Watch," because that's what this book and CD are supposed to make you want to do. Make no mistake, *Modeling the Dream CD* is a collection of sequential, rather than interactive, multimedia presentations that we want you to sit back and experience. So in one sense it's a book for the discerning PC-literate couch potato who's looking for a collection of killer multimedia.

   But *Modeling the Dream CD* can be much more than just a passive experience. Once you've been through The BigDemo and seen the best animations, you can read about how they were created. You'll also learn how we built a 3D environment with music and sound effects. If you are looking for even more depth, the underlying Grasp source code that holds everything together has been left open for you to read through and use. If you get stuck, just send me an email message and I'll see if I can help you out.

The Structure of This Book

The chapters in this book fall naturally into three sections: a discussion of the contents of the CD, a description of how we contructed The BigDemo and The SpaceBar, and a description of the demos that you can find on the disc and the artists who created them.

An Overview of the Disc

Chapter 1 introduces you to the multimedia software development field and briefly touches on the issue of copyright. The second chapter provides a detailed overview of the contents, layout, and use of the disc.

How We Built The BigDemos and The SpaceBar

In the third chapter you take a wild, half-hour long ride through a collection of flics to the accompaniment of music and sound effects. The second half of this chapter focuses on how to produce audio for multimedia. The fourth chapter looks at the creation of The SpaceBar, which is our own little interactive environment made with Autodesk 3D Studio.

Presenting the Works of Other Artists

The remaining three chapters present the works of the leaders in PC multimedia. Chapter 5 relates the experiences of the artists responsible for the flics. Chapter 6 is a guide to using the best demos we could find to drive your sound card in weird and wonderful ways, often to the accompaniment of mind-bending, high-speed graphics. Chapter 7 focuses on the bread and butter of the multimedia development world—general presentations.

In the three appendices you can look up the addresses and phone numbers of artists, find troubleshooting information, or obtain contact information about the many sources of material used in this book.

Read This Before Using the CD

Before you install *Modeling the Dream CD,* please take a moment to read this important information.

Hardware and System Requirements

The *Modeling the Dream CD* (MTD) requires a 386 PC compatible or better with 4MB total RAM, an SVGA graphics display, a hard drive with a minimum of 3MB of free space, and a Creative Labs Sound Blaster or compatible sound card. In addition to Sound Blaster compatibles, the General MIDI demos on the CD support virtually every sound board on the market, including cutting-edge wavetable boards like the Sound Blaster AWE and boards based on the Roland Sound Canvas.

MTD requires DOS 5 or better. To run some of the best demos, your system must be configured with *expanded memory* (EMS). To configure your system with expanded memory, you must use a memory manager, such as EMM386.EXE, which comes with DOS 5 or higher. To check whether your system is configured correctly, open your CONFIG.SYS file in a text editor (such as DOS EDIT) and look for a line that resembles this:

```
DEVICE=EMM386.EXE RAM
```

or this:

```
DEVICE=EMM386.EXE NOEMS
```

(The actual command in your CONFIG.SYS file may be somewhat longer—only the relevant parts have been shown here.) If this line contains NOEMS, you must delete NOEMS and replace it with the word RAM. If this line does not exist in your CONFIG.SYS file, you must add it. You must reboot your system before the change will take effect.

If you need further instructions, see your DOS manual. Another valuable resource is *Memory Management in a Multimedia World* (Waite Group Press, 1994, ISBN 1-878739-65-4).

Installation

For detailed installation instructions, see Chapter 2. If you are in a hurry to get started, follow these steps:

1. Insert the MTD CD in your CD-ROM drive and change to that drive. For example, if your CD-ROM drive is drive D, type

   `d:` (ENTER)

2. Type the following command at the DOS command prompt:

   `install` (ENTER)

3. Press a key corresponding to the drive on which you want to install the menu system.

4. Configure ANIPLAY for 640x480 screen resolution. (This program can be slow to load.)

5. Follow the instructions onscreen to select and test a MIDI driver for your sound card.

6. Follow the instructions onscreen to select and test a sampled sound driver for your sound card.

7. After you return to DOS, type the following to start MTD:

   `mtd` (ENTER)

The installation program, INSTALL.EXE, will create a \MTD subdirectory on your hard drive. The directory takes up nearly 3MB of disk space. INSTALL.EXE also creates an MTD.BAT file and writes it in the root directory of your hard disk.

While most of the demos are run directly off the CD, the menu system will automatically copy some of the demos onto your hard drive, because they need faster access time than the CD provides. These demos are copied into a \MTDTEMP directory. After you run one of these demos, the menu system gives you the option of deleting it to save hard disk space.

Creating and Using a Boot Disk

Some of the demos have special system requirements. To save you the trouble of reconfiguring your system to run these demos, we have provided the option of generating a boot disk. You will find this option on the SBDEMOS menu, which you can reach from the main menu that appears when MTD starts. After you have generated the boot disk, insert it in your A drive and press (CONTROL)-(ALT)-(DELETE) to reboot. After rebooting you will then see a menu from which you can run all of the demos that have special system requirements. For details, see Chapter 6.

Environment Space

You may get an error message if you attempt to start MTD without sufficient environment space. To increase your environment space, open your CONFIG.SYS file in a text editor and look for a line that resembles this:

```
SHELL=C:\DOS\COMMAND.COM  /E:512
```

The number after the /E: switch in this statement must be set to at least 512. Add the number 512 after the /E: or increase the value of the existing number, then save your CONFIG.SYS and reboot your computer.

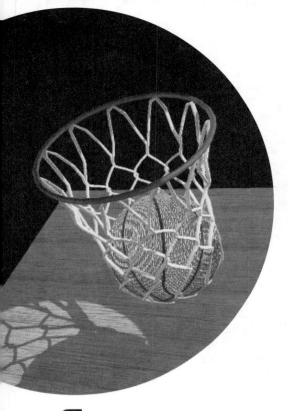

CHAPTER 1

Building
Our Dreams

F ew words are more ambiguous than *demo*. A computer demo can be almost anything: a
3D animation, an executable file coded in assembly language, or even a sales presentation.
And that's what makes demos so much fun: It's such a broad area that there is no telling
how it will be used to communicate ideas. Everything from cars to mutual funds, phone
services to virtual reality, all have benefited from some type of demo.

We prefer to think of this type of software as a new art form. But unlike works you'd
find in a museum, these pieces are relevant to the topics and products of today. Figures 1-1
through 1-3 are typical of the fun and interesting material we have to share with you. The
helicopter shown in Figure 1-1 is from a 25MB sequence of animations created by a student
just for fun. Figure 1-2 is a still frame from an animated proposal for a water sculpture. The
image of the funny-looking guy in the spacesuit in Figure 1-3 is pulled from the Waite
Group Press' Spring '94 CD-based catalog.

Unlike traditional art forms such as painting and sculpture, with art created on the PC
you can save your work at various stages and easily return to any point in your own creative
process. And the great thing is that exploring your creative talents doesn't require any special
equipment. You can probably use the same PC you now use for word processing and spread-
sheets to experiment with paint and animation programs.

Maybe you have already tried some of the freeware tools for building animations such
as POV-Ray or taken a stab at learning Autodesk Animator. Perhaps you dabble with other

1

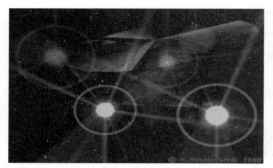

Figure 1-1 A close-up view of the helicopter from Mike Mulholland's HELLFIRE.FLI

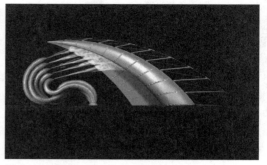

Figure 1-2 A side view of Pero Maticevic's water sculpture, The Blade

Figure 1-3 A screen from The Waite Group's spring catalog (modeling and rendering by Mike Miller)

systems and are just wondering where to direct your imagination next. Maybe you just like to watch the works of others. If any of the preceding is true, then this book should be right up your alley.

This book aims to inspire through example, because one of the best ways to learn how to create dazzling multimedia is to closely examine the work of others. Since most good ideas have to start somewhere and rarely spring to mind fully formed, consider this book a catalyst to spark your own creative reactions.

We have searched the globe through the avenues of email to find artists willing to share the fruits of their efforts. The offer of a library of Waite Group Press books to contributors has produced a wide-ranging collection of animated material. The openness with which our contributors shared their work and techniques is wonderfully refreshing. Perhaps this should be no surprise, as it is to everyone's benefit to pool a wealth of common experiences; by sharing ideas, everyone benefits.

The Three Types of Demo Makers

To better understand demos, let's first look at the three types of people who make them:

 Enthusiasts build animations and programs solely for the pride that comes from developing unique and innovative computer art. Money has absolutely nothing to do with many of the best demos ever created. There is a particularly interesting European phenomenon known as "The Demo Scene" in which groups compete against each other for prizes and respect. Kids as young as 14 join together, melding music and graphics into freeform productions that have an awe factor rivaling all but the most successful games-production houses. Waite Group Press is proud to have sponsored several of these competitions and continues to support these youngsters in their efforts to astound us with their creativity. We applaud them.

Professionals produce demonstrations as a service to their clients. Clients are driving this industry forward by expecting more sophisticated levels of interactivity, more radical graphic design, and most important, a more focused and coherent delivery of their message than ever before. A few years ago, all that was needed to sell a product was to have a message flash on the screen. That just doesn't cut it nowadays. The savvy multimedia buyer can tell a good demo or animated sequence from a bad one in a matter of seconds. To compete and survive in this business, you need to understand not just the underlying technology but also a myriad of other disciplines such as advertising, design, and typography.

Employees and small businesspeople learn to master the tools themselves, keeping production of their demos internal to their organizations. In general, these in-house users create graphics for presentation purposes while they continue to carry out their other jobs. For this reason, the most popular packages they use are Windows-based, where the speed of screen update isn't nearly as important as speed of creation and ease of delivery.

The only people who seem to dislike Windows these days are demo developers intent on maximizing the speed of screen updates. Few of the presentations included on the accompanying CD will even run under Windows, since they've been designed to directly control the hardware resources of the machine. We hope that you will find the effort of occasionally having to tweak the setup of your system to run a particular demo more than amply rewarded by the awesome sounds and graphics you will experience.

What Is The SpaceBar?

You may be aware that this book is a sequel to a previous collection called *Walkthroughs and Flybys CD*. Many readers of the first book requested more depth and insight into the creation of the showcased works. One problem that arose too often was that the techniques

Figure 1-4 The SpaceBar is an interactive 3D user interface to the vast collection of demos on the CD

employed by the contributors were so complex that to explain them briefly became impractical or meaningless. This is particularly true with the Sound Blaster demos, which for the most part are programmed in assembly language. Even with detailed information regarding the program structure and ample source code, only the most savvy programmer could glean a clue to the inner workings of these innovative young minds.

As a consolation prize, then, we offer you The SpaceBar, a screen from which is shown in Figure 1-4. The SpaceBar provides a 3D environment through which you can wander at will, choosing objects at random to run various demos. An in-depth case study documents the building of this interactive environment step-by-step in Chapter 4. You'll learn about the initial planning, 3D modeling, screen design, and Grasp programming. Don't expect a tutorial, but rather a summary of the various tasks and the processes that were used to create The SpaceBar.

Should you really want to dig deeper, all of the products used to create The SpaceBar are listed in Appendix C. In addition, most of the source files for The SpaceBar are included on the disc so that you can modify them in Grasp or Autodesk 3D Studio. If you choose to use any of The SpaceBar files in your own applications, please respect our efforts and credit the authors accordingly.

The Issue of Copyright: The graphics and programs on the accompanying disc are *not* in the public domain. Each piece has been contributed to *Modeling the Dream CD* on the condition that the artists be credited for their work and that the copyright remains fully and totally with them. Many of the contributing artists are full-time professionals in the demo business, for whom the production of computer art is their livelihood. You, as the purchaser of this book, are *not* free to use any of the graphics or sounds on the accompanying disc in your own projects without the permission of the contributing artist. If you enjoy a particular person's style and it is convenient for you to contact them, please do. Putting admirers and potential clients in touch with experts in the field is one of the main objectives of the *Walkthroughs and Flybys* series.

CHAPTER 2

An Overview of the CD

This chapter explains what you'll find on the CD and how to install it. First, you'll go through the installation process step-by-step. Next, you'll see how best to navigate through the material on the accompanying disc by using either of the two interfaces available to you. Investigating these two interfaces—The SpaceBar and the Automenu Interface—takes up the bulk of the chapter. Finally, you'll get a complete layout of the CD that explains how the contents are broken down into subdirectories, along with a large table listing everything on the disc.

 ## Installation

To get the show on the road place the disc in your CD-ROM drive and type

INSTALL (ENTER)

At the first prompt, press the letter of the drive onto which you would like to install the *Modeling the Dream CD* files. You will need around 3MB of hard disk space to hold the various files that need to reside on the hard disk. Only drive letters C: through F: are valid. You are given a final chance to confirm that both the source and target drives are correct before the installation program begins to copy files to a \MTD directory that the INSTALL creates on your hard disk.

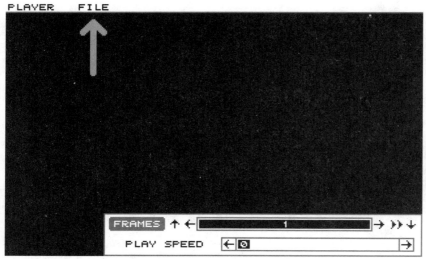

Figure 2-1 A screen from ANIPLAY.EXE with an arrow indicating the File menu

Configuring Autodesk ANIPLAY

Many of the flics on the CD are in 640x480 screen resolution. To view these SVGA animations, the Autodesk ANIPLAY runtime program has been chosen for its flexible and reliable operation. This stage of the installation process loads and configures ANIPLAY so that it runs in the correct video mode.

Once ANIPLAY has been loaded, select Screen Size from the File menu and then select a 640x480 screen driver. To help you find this, Figure 2-1 shows a screen shot of the ANIPLAY.EXE menu with an arrow pointing to the word *File* on the menu bar. When you quit the program, this configuration will be saved for all future sessions.

> If your PC doesn't present you with an option for a 640x480 screen driver under the ANIPLAY Screen Size menu, then you don't have a VESA driver installed. See Appendix B for information about VESA drivers.

Configuring Your Sound Card with MIDPAK and DIGPAK

Some of the most interesting parts of *Modeling the Dream CD* require drivers to be loaded resident in order to communicate with your sound card. The MIDPAK driver controls the playback of sequenced, MIDI music, while DIGPAK plays back sampled sounds. Each of these programs has a setup routine that will test your audio card before creating the driver

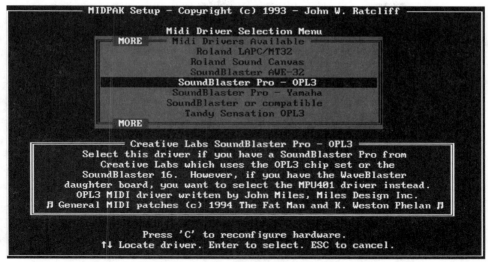

```
┌─────── MIDPAK Setup - Copyright (c) 1993 - John W. Ratcliff ───────┐
│                    Midi Driver Selection Menu                       │
│        ┌─ MORE ── Midi Drivers Available ──┐                        │
│        │          Roland LAPC/MT32          │                        │
│        │          Roland Sound Canvas       │                        │
│        │          SoundBlaster AWE-32        │                        │
│        │       SoundBlaster Pro - OPL3       │                        │
│        │       SoundBlaster Pro - Yamaha     │                        │
│        │     SoundBlaster or compatible      │                        │
│        │       Tandy Sensation OPL3          │                        │
│        └─ MORE ──────────────────────────────┘                        │
│   ┌══════ Creative Labs SoundBlaster Pro - OPL3 ══════┐              │
│   │  Select this driver if you have a SoundBlaster Pro from          │
│   │     Creative Labs which uses the OPL3 chip set or the            │
│   │   SoundBlaster 16.  However, if you have the WaveBlaster         │
│   │  daughter board, you want to select the MPU401 driver instead.   │
│   │  OPL3 MIDI driver written by John Miles, Miles Design Inc.       │
│   │ ♫ General MIDI patches (c) 1994 The Fat Man and K. Weston Phelan ♫│
│   └──────────────────────────────────────────────────────────────────┘
│                                                                      │
│                  Press 'C' to reconfigure hardware.                  │
│            ↑↓ Locate driver. Enter to select. ESC to cancel.         │
└──────────────────────────────────────────────────────────────────────┘
```

Figure 2-2 INSTALL runs SETM.EXE which tests your sound card and then creates a resident driver to control the playback of MIDI files

files. While you are running *Modeling the Dream CD* you won't need to worry about loading and unloading these drivers; the two user interfaces take care of all this for you.

The first step in the sound card setup procedure creates a directory called \MTD\TEMP into which all of the MIDPAK and DIGPAK files are unpacked. INSTALL then runs a program called SETM.EXE (see Figure 2-2) in which you select and test your sound card. Use the ⊙ and ⊙ keys to scroll through your choices. If you accidentally choose the wrong card you can press the (ESC) key to return to the scrolling list. The SETD.EXE program, which builds the audio driver, looks and feels just like SETM.EXE.

If you have a Sound Blaster card which is not installed on default settings, it is highly likely that your computer will hang if you choose to "AutoDetect" a Sound Blaster. After you press the (N) key to decline Autodetection, highlight the name of your card and press (C) to specify your soundcard settings. You will have to enter the I/O address and interrupt of your Sound Blaster. If you don't know what these are then you can figure them out by running the Creative Labs SBCONFIG.EXE or DIAGNOSE.EXE programs. See your sound card manual for further instructions.

Once the MIDPAK and DIGPAK drivers have been created, INSTALL moves them into the \MTD directory before deleting all unnecessary files in the \MTD\TEMP directory. The last screen in INSTALL.EXE notifies you that the installation was successful and instructs you to type **MTD** (ENTER) to load the user interface.

What INSTALL.EXE Does To Your PC

INSTALL creates a directory called \MTD and copies approximately 1.5MB of data into it. In addition, it creates a batch file called MTD.BAT in the root directory of the drive onto which you have installed these files. To load the menu interface, you type **MTD** (ENTER) from the DOS command line.

A number of the demonstrations on the CD will need access to your hard disk in order to run. There are several possible reasons for this. It may be that the system used to create the demo will attempt to write back files to its current directory, or that some characters used in the naming of the files aren't permissible under the CD-ROM formatting standard required by our replication facility. The important thing to remember is that all of the *Modeling the Dream CD* files will appear in just three places on your hard disk:

 MTD.BAT will be placed in the root directory.

 All of the main program files will be copied into \MTD.

Any temporary files will be copied into \MTDTEMP as you work your way through the disc.

Should you wish to remove *Modeling the Dream CD* from your hard disk, all you need to do is remove these two directories and delete the MTD.BAT file from the root directory.

 The Two Interfaces

Modeling the Dream CD is a bit like an art gallery, not just in being a collection of works, but also in how you can view the material. In The SpaceBar interface, you wander completely at random and trigger demos by clicking on graphical objects or *hotspots*. You can also use the MTD menuing system, which provides quick and orderly access to the material—much like looking up works of art in a museum guidebook.

The MTD Menuing System

The MTD menuing system is a flexible Navigation tool used to create the primary interface for *Modeling the Dream CD*. Its opening screen is shown in Figure 2-3. With the menuing program you can very quickly build a comprehensive interface to a vast number of programs. In a nutshell, this system works by writing out a DOS batch file and then terminating whenever a selection is made from one of the menus. After the program terminates, the new batch file executes a set of commands corresponding to your selection. When the batch file terminates, the MTD menuing system reloads. This program's ability to unload itself is perfect for any CD full of memory-hungry demos. There is a catch, however, with using this menu sys-

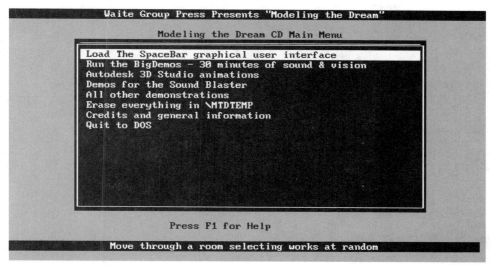

```
         Waite Group Press Presents "Modeling the Dream"

                    Modeling the Dream CD Main Menu
        ┌──────────────────────────────────────────────────┐
        │ Load The SpaceBar graphical user interface        │
        │ Run the BigDemos - 30 minutes of sound & vision   │
        │ Autodesk 3D Studio animations                     │
        │ Demos for the Sound Blaster                       │
        │ All other demonstrations                          │
        │ Erase everything in \MTDTEMP                       │
        │ Credits and general information                   │
        │ Quit to DOS                                       │
        │                                                  │
        │                                                  │
        │                                                  │
        │                                                  │
        └──────────────────────────────────────────────────┘

                        Press F1 for Help

         Move through a room selecting works at random
```

Figure 2-3 The initial screen from the MTD menuing system

tem for a CD: Because it is not possible to create files on a read-only device, the menu system first must be copied onto your hard disk. You can find it in the \MTD directory.

The MTD menuing system allows you to choose options from a list box displayed in the center of the screen. To select one of the menu items displayed in the list box, press the ⊕ or ⊕ key until you have highlighted the item you wish to select. To run the item, press (ENTER). Each menu item will either run a program or take you to a submenu.

You can exit the MTD menuing system any time by pressing (ALT)-(F4) To access the MTD menuing system's Help and information screens, press (F1) through (F4).

The SpaceBar Interface

To load The SpaceBar after it is installed, just press the (ENTER) key on the highlighted option in the main menu. The SpaceBar user interface performs the same basic functions as the MTD menuing system. When a hotspot is selected, the underlying Grasp program either plays an animation directly, or writes out a batch file and then terminates completely with the newly written batch file taking control.

Because Grasp was used to create this interface, you can not only load as many graphics and animations into memory as available RAM allows, but you can also have General MIDI music and digitized sound effects. The disadvantage to using a large application like The SpaceBar for a menu shell is that it takes much longer to reload than the tiny menuing program. Be prepared to wait a bit longer for The SpaceBar to reappear after watching demos than when using the MTD menuing system.

Figure 2-4 The SpaceBar user interface with messages visible in the status area

The SpaceBar Screen Layout

The lower-left area of the screen shown in Figure 2-4 always displays your current view of the room. Along the top of the screen is a box labeled *Available Demos from this View,* with messages describing the various items that you can select. If there are three items available for you to select given your current position and view, then three lines of text describing them appear in this box.

Along the right side of the screen is your Control Panel. The buttons let you change your view by turning to the left and right. The Map button displays a plan view of the room that takes up the entire screen when you press it. Your current position will be indicated with a flashing dot. You will also notice an Exit button that you can press to return to the Automenu interface.

The Location of Positions and Icons

There are eight positions in The SpaceBar from which you can select any of eight views, comprising a total of 64 different images you can interact with. As you can see from Figure 2-5, these positions are numbered from one to eight and are located roughly in the four corners of the room and along each of the four sides of the bar. You will also notice that there are a number of circles labeled A to Q, which denote hotspots that can be selected to trigger specific demos. Table 2-1 lists the demos that can be accessed from each of these icons.

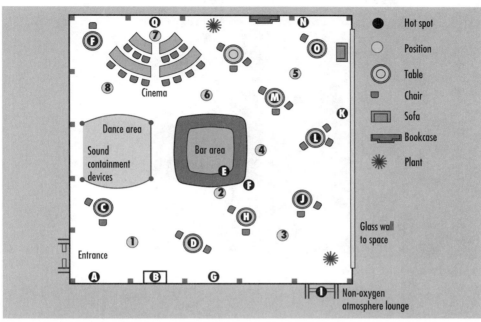

Figure 2-5 A plan view of The SpaceBar

Icon ref	The icon to be selected	Corresponding demos to be loaded
A	Old time movie machine	WGP Spring '94 Catalog—Shaddock
B	Doll house and globe	Nanotechnology Demo—Shaddock
C	Chess set	Chess II, Pinball, Helicopter—Mulholland
D	Lattice pyramid structure	Chernobyl encasement—Russam
E	Beer taps	The DMP BigDemo—Everybody!
F	Transparent bar post	Buckyball molecule—Richardson
G	Book on a pedestal	Crab-7—Reimann
H	Clock sitting on table	The Cuckoo Clock—Köhtz
I	Non-oxygen atmosphere room	Second Reality by The Future Crew
J	Table with morphing monitor	Hexpanding Universe—Young
K	Ship's helm	Starship Nightshift—Guthery
L	Translucent orb above table	Animations from Merlin Farmer
M	Table with morphing monitor	Radarsat—Meikle
N	Jukebox of old Wurlitzer type	Sound files—Boese
O	Table with morphing monitor	Kaleidosonics—Ratcliff and Wallace
P	Monitor comes out of table	Human motion study by Ingo Neuman
Q	A cinema with ten chairs	Making Movies contest entries

Table 2-1 Icons the user can select as referenced in Figure 2-5

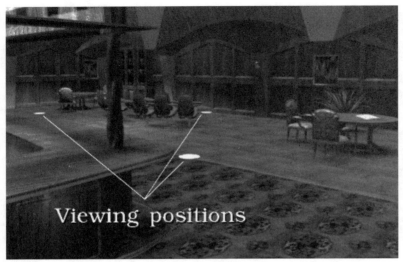

Figure 2-6 White discs on the floor indicate the positions in the room you can move to

Moving Around in The SpaceBar

You can move to an adjacent position by clicking your mouse over the bright white discs that you will find on the floor of the room, as can be seen in Figure 2-6. Chances are that you will need to swivel your view to either the left or right in order to find the next adjacent position or new hotspots. Do this by clicking your mouse over the corresponding arrows on the control panel located to the right of the SpaceBar image. You can also turn left or right by clicking the mouse along the extreme side of the screen.

 ## The Layout and Contents of the Disc

The purpose of this section is to give you a feel for the logic used in laying out the disc and its directory categories. A large table listing all of the files on the CD, their sizes, and the names of their creators can be found at the end of this chapter. Contact information for these artists can be found in Appendix A.

Be advised that material discussed in the following sections will be of interest only to readers who prefer to prowl around the disc manually. Users content to use the interfaces we have constructed should skip to Table 2-2.

The Root

In the root directory of the disc there are only two files. While the purpose of INSTALL.EXE is fairly obvious, you may not be aware of what TREEINFO.NCD does. Many PC users are completely reliant on the Norton Change Directory program, (NCD.EXE) to help them move around complex directory structures quickly. The TREEINFO.NCD file contains a map of the directory tree that can be accessed instantaneously by the NCD program, thereby facilitating manual navigation around the disc.

There are six subdirectories off of the root:

- \DEMOS   contains demos created using commercial authoring tools such as Grasp.

- \FLICS   provides all of the full-motion animations in the Autodesk FLI and FLC formats.

- \PROGRAMS   holds the various files required by the MTD user interface.

- \SBDEMOS   holds all of the custom-coded Sound Blaster demos.

- \SPACEBAR   contains the files needed for The SpaceBar user interface.

- \BIGDEMO   holds the music and sound effects for the grand tour.

The DEMOS Branch

Material off of the \DEMOS directory is subdivided based upon the last name of the contributor. For example, files sent in by Dr. Randale Sechrest can be found in the directory \DEMOS\SECHREST.

The FLICS Branch

The Autodesk flic format animations also have been grouped into subdirectories by artist name. In the \FLICS directory note the two script files ALLFLCS.SCR and ALLFLIS.AA. ALLFLCS.SCR is an ANIPLAY script file for playing all of the SVGA FLC animations. ALLFLIS.AA is an AAPLAY script file for playing all of the 320x200 animations. Files with an .AA extension are for AAPLAY and those with an .SCR are for ANIPLAY.

Each of the subdirectories off of \FLICS contain not just the flic files themselves, but also the requisite script files for playing the animations in that directory. The script files have been given the same name as the directory to make them easier to find should you be perusing the disc manually. For example, the disc has almost 100MB of 320x200 FLI files from Mike Mulholland. To play all of them in an endless loop, you would load the script file \FLICS\MULHOLLA\MULHOLLA.AA into AAPLAY. On the other hand, to play a script of SVGA animations by Pero Maticevic, you would load the script file \FLICS\MATICEVI\MATICEVI.SCR into ANIPLAY.

The PROGRAMS Branch

All the code for the user interface that is copied to your hard disk during installation originates from the \PROGRAMS directory. The .ZZZ files are MTD interface menu definition files. You can alter these *Modeling the Dream CD* menus by editing the .ZZZ files on your hard disk.

The SBDEMOS Branch

All of the custom-coded, really wacko stuff from the European Demo Scene is located here. As most of this material is distributed in compressed files via modem, we have elected to leave the files in their distributed format with the following exception: all archives have been converted to the ARJ format developed by Robert Jung (see Appendix C for more on ARJ). Also, any notices indicating the distribution routing of a demo (embedded by many electronic bulletin boards to advertise the existence of the board) have been removed. Every effort has been made to retain any informative files included by the original authors of these programs.

The SPACEBAR Branch

All of the Grasp, 3D Studio, and Animator Pro files for the creation of The SpaceBar user interface are located in the \SPACEBAR directory. They are described in detail in Chapter 3.

 # A List of the Contents of the CD

Tables 2-2, 2-3, and 2-4 list the entire contents of the *Modeling the Dream CD.* The three tables list, respectively, the general demonstrations, the 3D animations, and the Sound Blaster demos. Within each table, the demos are in alphabetical order by the creator's name.

Note that the third column of the tables lists the "core files" of the demonstration. These are the files that either execute the demo or contain the main body of the demo's executable code. In some cases where there is a set of several core files, DOS wildcards have been used. For example, MATICEVI.* means the set of files that begin with MATICEVI and have any filename extension. For more on wildcards, see your DOS documentation.

The fourth column of the table lists the approximate size of the demos in megabytes (MB). The size figures reflect the amount of space these files take up on the CD. Many of these demos are compressed into ARJ self-extracting files, particularly in the Sound Blaster demos section. To run these demos the interface will decompress them to the hard disk for you. A good general rule to follow is that when an ARJ file is decompressed, the decompressed files will occupy three times as much space as the ARJ file.

Creator or Team	Demo Title	Core Files	Size(MB)	MTD Address
Charles Jameson	Overview of Milligrid products	MINIFIT.BAT	0.7	DEMOS\JAMESON
Charles Jameson	Molex company overview	MOLEX.EXE	2.4	DEMOS\JAMESON
Karl Miller	Develcon Electronics looping demo	D-BRIDGE1.EXE	1.8	DEMOS\MILLER
Karl Miller	Marketing Systems demo	MARKETSY.EXE	1.9	DEMOS\MILLER
Karl Miller	Screen Resolutions demo	REZDEMO.EXE	301K	DEMOS\MILLER
Ian Powelly	Servomex 2500 demo	2500DEMO.EXE	1.44	DEMOS\POWELLY
Ian Powelly	Dr. Solomon's Anti-virus demo	AVDEMO.EXE	1.3	DEMOS\POWELLY
Ian Powelly	Watson Smith IP Converters	IPDEMO.EXE	0.71	DEMOS\POWELLY
Ian Powelly	Origa Shock Absorber demo	ORIGASAB.EXE	1.4	DEMOS\POWELLY
Ian Powelly	Large rotating molecule	BIGMOL.EXE	1.2	DEMOS\POWELLY
Ian Powelly	Bellis and Morcom Pump	PUMP.EXE	1.2	DEMOS\POWELLY
Ian Powelly	Servomex Emissions demo	EMISSION.EXE	2.39	DEMOS\POWELLY
Ian Powelly	ViglenTiko PC Guided Tour	VIGLEN.ARJ	2.87	DEMOS\POWELLY
Randale Sechrest	Medical Multimedia demo	MMGDEMO.BAT	0.66	DEMOS\SECHREST
Randale Sechrest	Treating Knee injuries	KNEE.BAT	0.59	DEMOS\SECHREST
Randale Sechrest	Patients Guide to Lower Back Pain	TREAT.BAT	2.59	DEMOS\SECHREST
Philip Shaddock	Nanotechnology Playhouse demo	NANO.EXE	1.85	DEMOS\SHADDOCK
Philip Shaddock	WGP Spring '94 catalog	CATALOG.BAT	69.4	DEMOS\SHADDOCK
Stephen Steininger	A rotating pipe created with Renderman	Q_PIPE.EXE	2.1	DEMOS\STEINING
Stephen Steininger	A chain link created with Renderman	Q_LINK.EXE	1.9	DEMOS\STEINING

Table 2-2 General demonstrations

Creator or Team	Demo Title	Core Files	Size(MB)	MTD Address
Jeff Alu	Animation of an office	ALU.SCR	7.3	FLICS\ALU
David Bleeker	Reflected water in a glass	GLASSP30.FLC	0.9	FLICS\MAKEMOVE
Contest entries	Miscellaneous raytraces at 640x480 resolution	MAKEMOVE.SCR	2.1	FLICS\MAKEMOVE
Contest entries	Miscellaneous raytraces at 320x200 resolution	MAKEMOVE.AA	4.0	FLICS\MAKEMOVE
Adrian Dodds	The can opener	CULINAIRE.FLC	2.1	FLICS\DODDS
Merlin Farmer	Miscellaneous logos and fun stuff	FARMER.AA	29.7	FLICS\FARMER
Tom Guthery	Mixing live video with Animator	STARSHIP.FLI	3.1	FLICS\GUTHERY
Henry Köhtz	The Cuckoo Clock	KOHTZ.AA	60.3	FLICS\KOHTZ
Chris Johnston	NASA animations	JOHNSTON.SCR	20.3	FLICS\JOHNSTON
Rick Lapidus	A basketball net	BALL4.FLC	4.60	FLICS\LAPIDUS
Pero Maticevic	Structural walkthroughs	MATICEVI.*	37.50	FLICS\MATICEVI
Bruce Meikle	A radar station	RADSAT5.FLI	2.20	FLICS\MEIKLE

continued on next page

continued from previous page

Creator or Team	Demo Title	Core Files	Size(MB)	MTD Address
Mike Mulholland	Killer Chess II	CHESS*.FLI	60.50	FLICS\MULHOLLA
Mike Mulholland	Follow a pinball around a table	PINBALL.FLI	19.67	FLICS\MULHOLLA
Mike Mulholland	The ultimate helicopter chase	HELLFIRE.FLI	33.40	FLICS\MULHOLLA
Grahame Naylor	Airplane takeoff and office	NAYLOR.AA	20.76	FLICS\NAYLOR
Ingo Neuman	A study in human motion	NEUMAN.AA	1.84	FLICS\NEUMANN
Thomas Reimann	Exciting space chase	CRAB7_CD.FLI	13.23	FLICS\REIMANN
Dan Richardson	Buckminsterfullerene molecule	BUCKA640.FLC	12.20	FLICS\RICHARDS
Jeff Rouyer	Animations created in POV-Ray	ROUYER.AA	17	FLICS\ROYER
Paul Russam	Encasing Chernobyl with robots	CHERNBOL.FLI	29.14	FLICS\RUSSAM
Chris Young	Hexpanding Universe	YOUNG.SCR	7.64	FLICS\YOUNG

Table 2-3 3D animations

Creator or Team	Demo Title	Core Files	Size(MB)	MTD Address
BrainBug	Great game preview	LOLLYPOP.EXE	0.45	SBDEMOS
BrainBug	Tiny intro but great	BRAINBUG.EXE	0.01	SBDEMOS
BrainBug	Turrican 3 demo 1	T3_1.EXE	0.63	SBDEMOS
BrainBug	Turrican 3 demo 2	T3_2.EXE	0.71	SBDEMOS
Cascada	Hex Appeal demo	APPEAL.EXE	0.33	SBDEMOS
DarkZone	Debut censored version	DZDEBUT.EXE	0.25	SBDEMOS
DarkZone	Gouroud shading in real time	GOURFACE.EXE	0.18	SBDEMOS
Epical	Takeover	TAKEOVER.EXE	0.69	SBDEMOS
Epical	Tangle	TANGLE.EXE	0.74	SBDEMOS
Future Crew	Chaotic Mind Music Disk	CHMIND.EXE	1.43	SBDEMOS
Future Crew	Second Reality	2NDREAL.EXE	2.07	SBDEMOS
Future Crew	The Journey Music Disk 1	JOURNEY1.EXE	0.85	SBDEMOS
Future Crew	The Journey Music Disk 2	JOURNEY2.EXE	1.01	SBDEMOS
Iguana	Inconexia—A Spanish group!	INCONEXI.EXE	0.48	SBDEMOS
Niko Boese	Miscellaneous WAV & VOC	none	6.12	SBDEMOS\BOESE
Rob Wallace	Kaleidosonics	KALEIDOS.EXE	0.88	SBDEMOS
Suprise!Productions	Copper—show VGA hardware effects	COPPER.EXE	0.15	SBDEMOS
Suprise!Productions	The Good, the Bad, and the Ugly	GOODBADU.EXE	0.55	SBDEMOS
Xography	Texture mapped graphics	ELEMENTS.EXE	1.43	SBDEMOS

Table 2-4 Sound Blaster demos

CHAPTER 3
The BigDemos

Modeling the Dream CD features two long sequences of animations accompanied by music, each using a different technique to drive your audio card. Together these "BigDemos" will last well over an hour. This chapter begins by showing you how to start these sequences from the menu system. In the pages that follow you will find brief descriptions of the 3D Studio, POV-Ray, and Polyray animations that are showcased in the BigDemos. In most instances these animations will be described more fully in Chapter 5, where they will be referenced under the last name of the contributor.

You'll then learn how both of the BigDemos were created. In the case of the DMP BigDemo, you'll find out how sequenced sampled instruments can be played behind animations using Otto Chrons' Dual MOD Player. In the case of the MIDPAK/DIGPAK BigDemo, you'll learn how we used extensions to Grasp—a script-based multimedia authoring system—to control digital audio and MIDI music simultaneously. These extensions, the MIDPAK and DIGPAK drivers, permit sound effects to be keyed to specific frames in the animation and delivered in such a way that the motion of the graphics is uninterrupted.

In the last section of this chapter, we'll discuss the various choices for multimedia sound playback, including Redbook audio, digital audio, MOD sequenced samples, and General MIDI. We'll also look at how these various approaches were implemented on *Modeling the Dream CD*.

Starting the BigDemos

To get rolling, just select *Run the BigDemos* from the Modeling the Dream main menu. At this screen you have the choice of running either the DMP BigDemo or the MIDPAK/DIGPAK BigDemo. After selecting either of these options, if you have sufficient disk space to hold the entire 140MB of graphics, you will be asked if you would like to download the entire dataset onto the faster medium of your hard drive. If your CD-ROM drive is only capable of sustaining a 150k/sec data transfer rate, we strongly recommend copying the dataset to your hard drive. Many of these animations exhibit a great deal of change from frame to frame and therefore run quite slowly from a single-speed CD-ROM drive. While either of the BigDemos are running you can skip ahead to the next flic by pressing the (ENTER) key. You can press (ESC) at any time to return to the menu system.

Highlights from the DMP BigDemo

All of the animations in this BigDemo are in the Autodesk .FLI file format at a resolution of 320x200. The music consists of original compositions by The Future Crew's "Skaven" and "Purple Motion." This section lists some of the highlights.

To help you find the animations on the disc, underneath each of the figures to the left of the page you will find the path and filenames of the flics described. Since they all start from the \FLICS directory, only the name of the second level directory is given. For example, in the case of the Waite Group Press logo that leads us off, the actual file path is \FLICS\MULHOLLA\WAITE.FLC, but to conserve space on the page and improve readability this has been truncated to MULHOLLA\WAITE.FLC. As elsewhere in this book, DOS wildcards are used when the animation consists of more than one "core" file. Thus HELLFIR?.FLI designates a set of files that begin with HELLFIR followed by any legal character plus the extension .FLI. See your DOS manual for details.

MULHOLLA\WAITE.FLC

An animated Waite Group Press Logo created by Mike Mulholland leads off The BigDemo. This is a relatively simple model consisting for the most part of standard geometric shapes which only took about two hours to create and render. The animated birdman sequence was created by Pat Nessling in Deluxe Paint Animation. A medley of the best animations, \FLICS\MEDLEY.FLC, then follows, giving you a preview of the best material on the disc.

If you are watching this flic from a single-speed CD-ROM drive it can stream painfully slowly. Remember, you can always press (ENTER) to advance to the next sequence.

MULHOLLA\HELLFIR?.FLI

Hellfire is one of the most awesome flics ever. You can read more about this 35MB sequence in Mike Mulholland's section in Chapter 5. One technique that Mike used very effectively in this animation involved applying a glass texture with additive transparency to a simple cone in 3D Studio.

MAKEMOVE\WHIRLI.FLI

This animation by Jeff Rouyer, A Whirligig is Born, won the Waite Group's *Making Movies on Your PC* contest. Using Polyray and some clever math, he created this dreamlike flic by breaking the animation into many separate scene files. The object movement code in each scene file picks up where the previous one leaves off. Whirligig is followed by Morpheus and Spin—these have to be among the most ingenious animations ever created in Polyray, in terms of both technique and imagination.

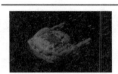

REIMANN\CRAB7.FLI

It took aspiring game animator Thomas Reimann over six months to create Crab7. One feature you might notice is how fast the spaceship moves across the screen at the end of the flic. The relatively small differences from frame to frame in this segment make a higher playback speed possible, because fewer pixels on the screen need to be updated.

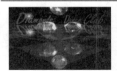

FARMER\DIAMONDS.FLI

Diamonds, by Merlin Farmer, shows off some of the clever things you can do with materials in 3D Studio Release 3. The texture of the glass has just the right degree of reflectiveness and transparency to simulate a waltzing diamond. Merlin created the small highlights that spin under the dance hall lights using an IPAS HiLite filter. (You can learn more about 3D Studio and IPAS in Chapter 4.)

NAYLOR\TAKEOFF.FLI

Grahame Naylor of Magic Lantern created this animation originally for broadcast video. He had to use a completely different background map for the sky than he used for the video version when rendering this animation to flic format. The background for the video version required too many colors when rendered as a flic, which left the airplane looking rough and contoured.

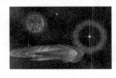

GUTHERY\STARSHIP.FLI

Tom Guthery made Starship Nightshift completely in Animator Pro. He created the brilliant effect of the small planet surface by recording swirling food dye in a glass with a ComputerEyes RT video capture card.

MEIKLE\RADSAT5.FLI

Bruce Meikle of Fire Media produced this animation of a radar track-ing station for the Canadian Space Agency. He created the yellow beams by using a flic as an animated opacity map to vary the trans-parency of a cylinder linked to the dish. A more detailed description of this technique can be found on page 68 of *Walkthroughs and Flybys CD* under the heading *Simulating Explosions without IPAS*.

 # Highlights of the MIDPAK/DIGPAK BigDemo

The second BigDemo uses an entirely different technology to drive your sound card. When you execute the menu selection *Run the MIDPAK/DIGPAK BigDemo* you may notice that two programs, MIDPAK and DIGPAK are loaded into memory before the Grasp runtime engine is loaded. MIDPAK controls how music is played, while DIGPAK handles sound effects. If you have a Sound Blaster compatible or another card only capable of FM synthesis, be prepared for a level of musical quality somewhat below what DMP delivers. However, if you have a wavetable sound card such as the Sound Blaster AWE or a card based on the Roland Sound Canvas, then MIDPAK will deliver excellent music.

One great thing that this BigDemo has to offer is the ability to play sound effects keyed to a particular frame of an animation. In the first flic, Mike Mulholland's Killer Chess II, you'll notice that dozens of different sound effects punctuate movements, collisions, and explosions as this brutal chess game is played out. Because each sound effect file is loaded into RAM by Grasp before the flic begins, there is no disruption in the smoothness of the animation when the sound effect is delivered. Because the seek time of the laser in a CD-ROM drive is so slow, if each sound effect had to be loaded just before it was played then these animations would be interrupted constantly.

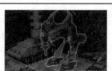

MULHOLLA\CHESS??.FLI

Killer Chess II is a monster animation with too many effects to even begin to list. It boggles the mind that Mike Mulholland was able to create this flic on a machine with only 8MB of RAM and a 200MB hard disk. Tim Melton arranged the MIDI sequence for this flic, a Bach concerto that plays softly in the background, mitigating the effect of the carnage onscreen only slightly.

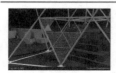

RUSSAM\CHERNOB?.FLI

This scaled-down version of a proposal for encasing the leaking Chernobyl nuclear reactor with robots has attracted the attention of political leaders in several countries. The team at the Electric Drawing Board share their story of combining environmental protection, politics, and multimedia in the Paul Russam section of Chapter 5.

NEUMAN*.FLI

This study of human motion created by Ingo Neuman really shows off the power of hierarchical linking in 3D Studio. Notice how smoothly the whole figure walks with each segment of each limb coordinated perfectly.

KOHTZ\CAM*.FLI

Henry Köhtz's cuckoo clock sequence in its entirety weighs in at a hefty 58MB and alone would run for ten minutes on an average CD-ROM drive. This animation starts off a bit slowly if you have a short attention span, but stay with it, because it has some lovely sequences.

How the DMP BigDemo Works

DMP, which plays the incredible multitrack S3M music in this BigDemo, has a resident mode in which it can run a batch file while continuing to play music in the background. On a 486/66 machine it appears to take only about 1/4 of the CPU resources and, provided that expanded memory (EMS) is available, around 200K of conventional RAM.

The DMP BigDemo calls two batch files one after the other, passing new parameters through DOS environment variables. The only problem with this technique is that it's very memory-intensive. As long as your system is configured to have at least 520K of conventional DOS memory and 512K of expanded memory (EMS), everything will run fine. If you don't have EMS, DMP will load the music files into conventional memory leaving too little RAM to play the animations. If you are not sure whether you have EMS memory, open your CONFIG.SYS file in a text editor such as DOS EDIT and look for a line that resembles this:

```
DEVICE=EMM386.EXE
```

If you see the word NOEMS on that line, you will need to delete it, replace it with the word RAM, save your CONFIG.SYS file, then press (CONTROL)-(ALT)-(DELETE) to reboot your system. If you don't have this line in your CONFIG.SYS file, you need to add it.

The DMP BigDemo is controlled by a DOS batch file written out by the *Modeling the Dream CD* menuing system. When the user selects *Run the DMP BigDemo,* the commands inside the BIGDEMO.ZZZ menu definition file are written out to a temporary batch file that begins to execute. For each song in DMP BigDemo, you will find six corresponding lines in the ZZZ file resembling these:

```
+set fpat=\flics
+set flcs=medley.flc
+set tune=aqua.s3m
+call pmod.bat
+if exist abort goto end
+tpicem /w:300 /e /k /v:l %c%\bigdemo\mulholla.gif >nul
```

You can find the complete file in your \MTD directory. Here is a description of what this file does:

 The first three lines set environment variables to hold the directory name containing the flics, the names of the flics to be run, and the song to be played.

 The next line calls the batch file PMOD.BAT to start the music.

 When the music is finished, the next line checks for the existence of a small file signaling that the user aborted.

 The last line in the cycle displays a credit screen with the name of the next artist.

PMOD.BAT, which controls music playback, is shown here:

```
crankup /p
dmp -x -wpflc.bat %c%\bigdemo\%tune%
exit
```

When PMOD.BAT is called a small Grasp program, CRANKUP.EXE is executed to raise the volume levels of the Sound Blaster mixer to near maximum. (Technically, this only applies to the Sound Blaster Pro and later versions. The original Sound Blaster had no onboard mixer to allow programmatic adjustment of volume levels.) Next DMP is executed in resident mode. It spawns yet another DOS session to run the PFLC.BAT file, shown here:

```
@echo off
%c%
cd %fpat%
%t%readflic %flcs%
%t%
if errorlevel 1 goto ab
goto jump
:ab
echo abort >abort
:jump
fadedown /p
68
exit
```

PFLC.BAT changes the current directory from the hard disk to the appropriate directory on the CD and executes a flic player called READFLIC.EXE, which plays the animations listed in the *flcs* environment variable one after another. The source code for READFLIC.EXE was provided by Jim Kent, the author of Animator Pro, but some modifications were necessary so that the program would generate an ERRORLEVEL code so that we could have it terminate when the user presses (ESC). (You can find the original and the modified Borland C++ source code in the file \PROGRAMS\SOURCE\READFLIC.ARJ.)

After READFLIC.EXE terminates, the ERRORLEVEL of the program is checked by DOS. If the user pressed (ESC) to quit, a small file is written back to the hard disk signaling that an abort has been requested. Finally, FADEDOWN.EXE is run to gently lower the mixer volume level. Just before we EXIT a tiny program called 68.EXE is executed. This generates an ERRORLEVEL of 68, indicating to the resident DMP program that it is to quit immediately rather than returning to the tracker interface upon closing its spawned DOS session. After this PMOD.BAT's EXIT command passes control back to the batch file originally written out by the menuing system.

Using the IF EXIST command, the batch file generated by the menuing system checks to see if (ESC) was pressed during the playback of the animations, by checking for the ABORT file created by PFLC.BAT. If ABORT does not exist, then the PICEM program by John Bridges is executed to display a screen with the name of the next artist and the animations about to be shown. PICEM takes two command-line switches:

 The /W:200 switch tells it to wait for a period of 2 seconds.

 The /K switch means to proceed without a key being pressed.

After that the process repeats itself over and over until the DMP BigDemo is finished, at which time the environment variables are cleared before the menuing system again reloads.

If you want to change the DMP BigDemo to add your own animations and MOD files, just edit the BIGDEMO.ZZZ menu file. If you make a mistake and the menu system fails you can get the original BIGDEMO.ZZZ file from the \PROGRAMS directory on the CD.

How the MIDPAK/DIGPAK BigDemo Works

The MIDPAK/DIGPAK BigDemo was created in Grasp, a powerful script-based DOS multimedia authoring system. We've given you the opportunity to examine and modify this BigDemo as well by leaving all of the Grasp source code completely open. When you installed *Modeling the Dream CD,* the main Grasp program file, BIGDEMO.TXT, was copied into the \MTD directory of your hard disk where it is just waiting for you load it into a text editor. Experienced Grasp users should be able to add their own flics, music, and sound effects to the MIDPAK/DIGPAK BigDemo if they read through the next few pages and spend some time looking over the comments in the BIGDEMO.TXT file.

If you have never used Grasp, the next few pages will give you a feel for the power of the system, but they are not by any means a keystroke-by-keystroke tutorial. For that you should get *Multimedia Creations* by Philip Shaddock (Waite Group Press, 1992, ISBN 1-878739-26-3).

Initial Execution Conditions

Usually all of the files for a demo are contained in a single Grasp library file (.GL). But because we wanted to leave all of the source code for this demo open and accessible to you, its .GL contains only a single text file with just two lines of code:

```
closegl                    ;close BIGDEMO.GL
link @t$"\mtd\bigdemo.txt" ;continue execution with BIGDEMO.TXT
```

The *closegl* statement tells Grasp to close the library file and begin loading its instructions from DOS text files. In this case the file is \MTD\BIGDEMO.TXT, located on your hard disk, so we need to tell Grasp where this drive is. This is done by preceding the path specification for this program file with a drive letter that is contained in the variable *t*. This is a DOS environment variable holding the drive letter of the hard disk onto which you have installed *Modeling the Dream CD*. For example if you have installed *Modeling the Dream CD* to your C drive then Grasp will look for the file C:\MTD\BIGDEMO.TXT. Similarly, a variable *c* contains the drive letter of your CD-ROM drive. These environment variables are set by the MTD.BAT file which you run every time you load the initial MTD system. If you wish to run BIGDEMO.TXT from within the Grasp editor (GraspC.EXE) you must first set the environment variables *t* and *c* to the values assigned in your MTD.BAT file.

BigDemo Program Structure

The code structure for The MIDPAK/DIGPAK BigDemo is organized into a set of subroutines that are listed in a data table identified by the label *playlist:*, shown here:

```
playlist:
chess
chernob
pinball
neuman
melon
grafton
kohtz
end
```

After each successive subroutine is processed, control is returned to the main loop and a counter is incremented. This counter, which is held in the variable *cnt,* is then used with the *dataskip* command to advance through the list of subroutines and obtain the name of the next procedure to run. If the name of the subroutine happens to be *end,* then the end of the list has been reached, which results in *cnt* being set back to 0, effectively passing execution back to the first subroutine. This causes The BigDemo to loop until a user presses the (ESC) key. This linked list implementation allows for the easy organization of code into manageable subroutines, and makes it very easy to change the order of the animations in the demo. Try it yourself: Just open BIGDEMO.TXT in DOS EDIT, search for *playlist:*, and reorder the list. Save the file and then run MTD. You will find that the order of the animations has been customized.

These next lines of code comprise the main program loop:

```
top:
  databegin playlist    ;open datalist
  dataskip @cnt         ;skip to next procedure
  set sub @             ;store subroutine name in variable sub
  if @sub=="end"        ;have we advanced past the last sub?
    set cnt 0           ;yes, so start again
```

```
  goto top              ;jump to top
 endif
 @sub                   ;execute sub
 fadedown               ;fade down the music
  set cnt @cnt+1        ;increment cnt
goto top                ;end of main
```

Each of the subroutines listed in *playlist:* first starts the General MIDI music before calling a parsing routine that reads in a file list and an effects table. A MIDI sound track is started by passing the name of the sound file to the resident MIDPAK driver through the interface provided by the MIDPAK.GRP Grasp extension. Sound cards relying on the OPL3 chip, such as the Sound Blaster, Gravis UltraSound, and Adlib, will be passed General MIDI files with the extension .OPL. Sound cards utilizing wavetable synthesis, such as the Sound Blaster AWE, Wave Blaster, and Roland MPU401, will run General MIDI files with the .GEN extension.

The MIDPAK and DIGPAK Drivers

One of Grasp's most interesting and little-used features is its expandability via programs that link with it at runtime. With this feature, programmers can develop their own Grasp modules (GRPs) and call them from within Grasp. This allows multimedia developers to use loads of different hardware and software with Grasp without waiting for a new version which may or may not contain the necessary support. Sample applications that use GRPs are drivers for laser printers, touch screens, video overlay cards, and of most interest to us, sound cards.

Grasp's standard sound capabilities are very limited, so to create this version of The BigDemo, Jason Gibbs at IMS wrote a GRP to provide an interface to the DIGPAK and MIDPAK drivers. These powerful device-independent sound card drivers were developed by John Miles and John Ratcliff and are available from The Audio Solution (you can find more information in Appendix C). These drivers provide superb quality sound and MIDI playback on a wide range of sound boards and have been used with great success in a wide variety of computer games such as 7th Guest and Seawolf, to name a couple.

The following Grasp program demonstrates how easy it is to play General MIDI and sampled sound files simultaneously with flic files.

```
load midpak.grp            ; load the MIDPAK.GRP program into Grasp
load digpak.grp            ; load the DIGPAK.GRP program into Grasp
video s                    ; select Super VGA 640x480 256 color graphics
midpak use backgrnd.xmi    ; indicate the General MIDI file to play
midpak play                ; start playing the MIDI file
digpak use sample.raw      ; indicate sampled sound effect file to play
digpak play                ; start playing the sound effect file
putdff cuckhoo.flc         ; start playing an animation file
```

Having the capability to play music and sound effects is only half the battle. However, to produce great multimedia you need to have great audio, which is Rob's area of expertise. Much of what follows was originally written by Rob before being reorganized for inclusion in this book. Rob Wallace is one of the multimedia industry's leading composers. His credits

Figure 3-1 Multimedia Kaleidosonics
is Rob Wallace's latest creation

include The Miracle Piano Teaching System, Tom Landry Strategy Football, MIG29, Seawolf, and Mario's Missing Deluxe. In 1993 Rob released Multimedia Kaleidosonics (a screen from which can be seen in Figure 3-1) which is his first interactive album created with programming guru John Ratcliff. Don't miss the awesome demo for this product that you can find described in Chapter 6.

 # Music and Sound Alternatives

In this section of *Modeling the Dream CD,* you'll learn about several alternatives for playing music and sound in a multimedia production. All of these solutions, with the exception of Redbook audio, are implemented on the CD, so you'll be able to compare them directly, as well as read about their technical virtues and shortcomings.

Redbook Audio Is the Best You Can Get

The best audio you can get from a CD drive is known as *Redbook* audio, which is the same format found on conventional audio CDs that you buy at your music retailer. Unfortunately, when the CD drive is in Redbook mode, it has to be dedicated to playing Redbook audio and can't run flics or access any other type of data. We could have copied a number of flic files from the CD to the hard disk allowing them to be displayed while the CD was in Redbook mode, but there would be some real disadvantages to doing this. First, you would need a hard disk large enough to hold hundreds of megabytes of flics. You would also need a great deal of patience while you waited for these files to be copied from the CD to your hard disk. Still worse, because Redbook audio requires a staggering 10MB of storage per minute, we would have had to cut way back on the number of flics on the disc in order to make room for the audio.

In certain cases, combining flics with Redbook audio works great. Generally, if the specification for a project gives you the latitude to consume large amounts of disk space, provides you with time to download the data before the presentation is shown, and requires the fastest possible animation and highest quality sound, then Redbook is a good choice. If, however, a demo needs to run on demand from a CD or if disk space or available memory is a constraint, then there are other alternatives.

Digitized Sound Files

Digitized, or sampled, sound is the most common way of providing music, speech, and sound effects in multimedia productions. This format is simply an audio recording in digital form that can be played back through your sound board. The fidelity of the recording depends on the sample size (8- or 16-bit) and the sampling rate (the number of times an audio signal is sampled each second). *Modeling the Dream CD* uses 8-bit 11Khz and 22Khz samples. While normally not as memory-hungry as Redbook audio data, these files still use up a lot of memory, especially if they are longer than 20 or 30 seconds. Using samples too large to fit into available RAM causes the sound to break up while it is being loaded off the CD.

In the MIDPAK/DIGPAK BigDemo, digitized sound is synchronized to specific frames in the animation to provide sound effects while MIDI music plays simultaneously in the background. This enables precise timing of the sound effects, independent of the playback speed of the flic, as long as the sound effect is not so long that it continues after the visual event to which it has been synchronized has passed.

Digitized sound is also used in the fly-in to The SpaceBar. The approach used there is the similar to what was done on the original *Walkthroughs and Flybys CD*. A sample in the Creative Labs .VOC format plays, and when it is finished playing a section of the .VOC sound file, is set to repeat. (You can set repeat loops using the VEDIT2.EXE utility that ships with the Sound Blaster.) If the sound finishes before the animation, the repeat block keeps playing until the animation comes to an end. This assures that music will play continuously regardless of the flic playback speed. The problem with repeat blocks is that they can become extremely repetitive during a long animation.

MOD Sequenced Samples

MOD, S3M, and related technologies use small samples as a set of instruments, setting the pitch, volume, and other parameters of the sounds to create multichannel music. The DMP BigDemo was created using Otto Chrons' Dual MOD Player to play back MOD and S3M files. Because MOD files originated on the Amiga, they originally could have up to four channels reflecting the four independent channels for digitized audio in the hardware of the Amiga. A MOD file is almost always much larger than a MIDI file because it contains a sample of the instrument; however, because MOD technology "reuses" small instrument samples to create a full range of notes, MOD files are far more compact than digital audio files. MOD technology essentially turns your sound board into a multitrack sample player—something that would normally require you to purchase expensive hardware.

The DMP BigDemo plays S3M files composed by The Future Crew's Jonne Valtonen and Peter Hajba using their Scream Tracker 3 music composition software. The only real difference between MOD and S3M is that S3M files can have up to 16 channels. If you want to check out Scream Tracker 3 you can find it in \SBDEMOS\SCRNT301.EXE.

Musical Instrument Digital Interface

MIDI stands for Musical Instrument Digital Interface. Think of it as a standard language that allows digital devices to talk among themselves. A MIDI file contains only data instructions and values that, when played through a MIDI device like a sound card, will reproduce the song. MIDI came about when a few keyboard design technicians from several synthesizer manufacturers got together to explore methods of making keyboards talk to each other. Their results were revealed at the first North American Music Manufacturers show in Los Angeles in 1983. They showed how two different synthesizers connected together with cables could be played simultaneously. The audience was amazed, and MIDI was born.

A MIDI device is any piece of hardware that can send, receive, or pass on MIDI data. Examples would be a MIDI keyboard, a PC sound card with a MIDI interface, or even a sophisticated theater lighting console that can receive MIDI data to cue lights or trigger a fogger.

MIDI Data

MIDI data is carried in bytes that fall into two categories: instructions and values. By using a combination of bytes, a tremendous variety of information can be exchanged between two MIDI devices. The first byte in any MIDI sequence is the *status byte,* which is used to call a function. Encoded in the status byte is the MIDI channel, of which there are 16 in the MIDI specification. Until a different status byte is received, all information goes into that channel. As you can see from the illustration in Figure 3-2, the Note on status byte tells the

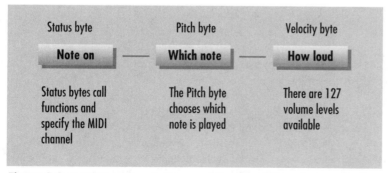

Figure 3-2 A MIDI note requires a minimum of three bytes: the first turns on the note, the second determines the note's pitch, and the final byte, called velocity, determines how loud it is played

MIDI device to sound a note, but two more bytes are needed to actually make something happen. The *pitch byte* tells the MIDI device which note to play, and the *velocity byte* tells the device how loud to play it. Velocity ranges from 0 to 127 where zero is silence and a value of 127 is the maximum volume.

Rob's primary tool for authoring a MIDI file is a Roland Sound Canvas SC-55. When his software issues the bytes to trigger the sound of a particular instrument, what he hears is a very close approximation of the instrument. This approximation, created by a process called wavetable synthesis, is based on a sample of the actual sound stored on a chip in his Roland Sound Canvas. The wave table contains information regarding the attack and decay rates of the sound's waveform. An aspect of the sampled sound is played back and the rest of the sound is reconstructed algorithmically.

The General MIDI Specification

General MIDI is really just an extension to the MIDI standard that provides for a set patch map. A set patch map means that the instrument corresponding to each patch number is standardized, so that it will be the same on any playback device. On a General MIDI device, patch 1 is always a grand piano, patch 67 is always a tenor sax, and so forth. General MIDI support was made part of the MPC standard to ensure that music in the MIDI format will sound the same across a wide variety of hardware. The General MIDI standard instruments are shown in Table 3-1.

Piano		Organ		Bass	
1	Acoustic Grand	17	Drawbar Organ	33	Acoustic Bass
2	Bright Acoustic	18	Percussive Organ	34	Electric Bass (finger)
3	Electric Grand	19	Rock Organ	35	Electric Bass (pick)
4	Honky-Tonk	20	Church Organ	36	Fretless Bass
5	Electric Piano 1	21	Reed Organ	37	Slap Bass 1
6	Electric Piano 2	22	Accordion	38	Slap Bass 2
7	Harpsichord	23	Harmonica	39	Synth Bass 1
8	Clav	24	Tango Accordion	40	Synth Bass 2

Chromatic Percussion		Guitar		Strings	
9	Celesta	25	Acoustic Guitar (nylon)	41	Violin
10	Glockenspiel	26	Acoustic Guitar (steel)	42	Viola
11	Music Box	27	Electric Guitar (jazz)	43	Cello
12	Vibraphone	28	Electric Guitar (clean)	44	Contrabass
13	Marimba	29	Electric Guitar (muted)	45	Tremolo Strings
14	Xylophone	30	Overdriven Guitar	46	Pizzicato Strings
15	Tubular Bells	31	Distortion Guitar	47	Orchestral Strings
16	Dulcimer	32	Guitar Harmonics	48	Timpani

continued on next page

continued from previous page

Ensemble

49	String Ensemble 1
50	String Ensemble 2
51	SynthStrings 1
52	SynthStrings 2
53	Choir Aahs
54	Voice Oohs
55	Synth Voice
56	Orchestra Hit

Brass

57	Trumpet
58	Trombone
59	Tuba
60	Muted Trumpet
61	French Horn
62	Brass Section
63	SynthBrass 1
64	SynthBrass 2

Reed

65	Soprano Sax
66	Alto Sax
67	Tenor Sax
68	Baritone Sax
69	Oboe
70	English Horn
71	Bassoon
72	Clarinet

Pipe

73	Piccolo
74	Flute
75	Recorder
76	Pan Flute
77	Blown Bottle
78	Skakuhachi
79	Whistle
80	Ocarina

Synth Lead

81	Lead 1 (square)
82	Lead 2 (sawtooth)
83	Lead 3 (calliope)
84	Lead 4 (chiff)
85	Lead 5 (charang)
86	Lead 6 (voice)
87	Lead 7 (fifths)
88	Lead 8 (bass+lead)

Synth Pad

89	Pad 1 (new age)
90	Pad 2 (warm)
91	Pad 3 (polysynth)
92	Pad 4 (choir)
93	Pad 5 (bowed)
94	Pad 6 (metallic)
95	Pad 7 (halo)
96	Pad 8 (sweep)

Synth Effects

97	FX 1 (rain)
98	FX 2 (soundtrack)
99	FX 3 (crystal)
100	FX 4 (atmosphere)
101	FX 5 (brightness)
102	FX 6 (goblins)
103	FX 7 (echoes)
104	FX 8 (sci-fi)

Ethnic

105	Sitar
106	Banjo
107	Shamisen
108	Koto
109	Kalimba
110	Bagpipe
111	Fiddle
112	Shanai

Percussive

113	Tinkle Bell
114	Agogo
115	Steel Drums
116	Woodblock
117	Taiko Drum
118	Melodic Tom
119	Synth Drum
120	Reverse Cymbal

Sound Effects

121	Guitar Fret Noise
122	Breath Noise
123	Seashore
124	Bird Tweet
125	Telephone Ring
126	Helicopter
127	Applause
128	Gunshot

Drum Sounds Key#

35	Acoustic Bass Drum
36	Bass Drum 1
37	Side Stick
38	Acoustic Snare
39	Hand Clap
40	Electric Snare
41	Low Floor Tom
42	Closed Hi-Hat
43	High Floor Tom
44	Pedal Hi-Hat
45	Low Tom
46	Open Hi-Hat
47	Low-Mid Tom
48	Hi-Mid Tom
49	Crash Cymbal 1
50	High Tom
51	Ride Cymbal 1
52	Chinese Cymbal
53	Ride Bell

Drum Sounds Key# (continued)

54	Tambourine	64	Low Conga	74	Long Guiro
55	Splash Cymbal	65	High Timbale	75	Claves
56	Cowbell	66	Low Timbale	76	Hi Wood Block
57	Crash Cymbal 2	67	High Agogo	77	Low Wood Block
58	Vibraslap	68	Low Agogo	78	Mute Cuica
59	Ride Cymbal 2	69	Cabasa	79	Open Cuica
60	Hi Bongo	70	Maracas	80	Mute Triangle
61	Low Bongo	71	Short Whistle	81	Open Triangle
62	Mute Hi Conga	72	Long Whistle		
63	Open Hi Conga	73	Short Guiro		

Table 3-1 The General MIDI instrument patch specification

Note that drum sounds occur on channel 10 only in the General MIDI specification. Drum sounds are distributed over the keys of a musical keyboard within a single channel in order to conserve space. To understand this, consider that a piano or a clarinet has only one essential sound that occurs at a great number of pitches, whereas the sounds made by drums have many different essential sounds that are each played at a single pitch. This makes it convenient to combine these sounds into one channel and assign each of them to an individual key.

Frequency Modulation or FM Synthesis

When you listen to an instrument you might be hearing it through any number of sound cards ranging from the ancient Adlib through to an Ensoniq SoundScape. For each card to make that sound, it has to have a General MIDI wavetable synthesis chip on board that plays back a representation of the sampled sound, or it must have the Yamaha 0PL2 or OPL3 FM Chip on board to play a synthesized version of the instrument. While FM synthesis through the OPL3 chip is an inexpensive and efficient way to reproduce the sounds of musical instruments, it is woefully lacking in acoustic accuracy. A clarinet or a flute may sound fairly close to the real thing through an OPL3 chip, but a grand piano, timpani set, or cymbal crash won't sound anything like the genuine article. In short, wavetable synthesis means that you hear a reconstructed approximation of an actual sample of the musical instrument, while FM synthesis reproduces a frequency-modulated version of the musical instrument which sounds electronic rather than natural.

MIDPAK Drivers and the Extended MIDI Format

Since there are more than 16 different sound cards that can play MIDI, developing drivers for all these cards would require a great deal of effort. To get around that problem we used the MIDPAK set of programming tools that contains all the drivers for all the major and minor sound cards made. MIDPAK is actually a scaled-down version of the AIL System developed by John Miles, which is used by many game developers to solve the problems of implementing MIDI music in games. MIDPAK utilizes a specially compiled version of the popular type 1 MIDI files that usually have a .MID extension. These files are known as eXtended MIDI files and normally have the extension .XMI. To account for the differing capabilities of FM and wavetable synthesis on the *Modeling the Dream CD,* the eXtended MIDI files in the \BIGDEMO directory have either .OPL extensions (if they are for use with FM synthesis sound cards) or .GEN extensions (if they have been optimized for wavetable synthesis).

One of the programs that comes with MIDPAK is a utility that takes the .MID file and rearranges it into a .XMI file by further condensing the data stream and adding hooks for file markers and channel attributes. These additional features allow the computer musician to program the file so that the song will loop in different ways or even switch channels on the fly. The channel switching feature is particularly relevant to game play. For example, imagine that you are playing a war game flying in a jet with the music cranking along in a major key with upbeat percussion. All of a sudden, you're hit or playing badly and a "call" from the program will cause the eXtended MIDI file to swap channels. The percussion becomes subdued and the melody and accompaniment part, formerly in a major key, now play the same song in a minor mode, which is quite effective in producing a "seamless" mood change.

The Advantages of Extended MIDI as Compared to .CMFs or .ROLs

In 1987 a Canadian by the name of Henry Chalifour wrote a program called Visual Composer that made it possible to play music through the Adlib card. Mostly because it was unique, being the first sound card on the market, the Adlib became the first popular PC sound card. Visual Composer introduced .ROL files that, although sequenced like a MIDI file, contained absolutely minimal information. The Creative Labs .CMF file format is very similar to .ROL except that it has a different file header. In essence, these formats are dinosaurs, limited to playing back either nine notes at a time in melodic mode or six notes at a time in percussive mode. With MIDPAK you can play up to 32 notes at a time in addition to having all the other technical benefits of loop marking, channel swapping, and quantization.

 # In Closing

PC audio technology is continuing to advance in leaps and bounds. Recently, the Sound Blaster AWE has been released, offering everything a sound card ever had, along with the capabilities of the most advanced synthesizers. From their competitors, Media Vision, a new technology known as "wave guide" looms just over the vaporware horizon that claims to let you introduce the randomness of natural sounds into your computer applications. But audio isn't the only technology to have reached maturity in the multimedia game. Read on and enter the world of The SpaceBar, a 3D environment created by CAD and visualization expert Simon Browne.

CHAPTER 4

Building
The SpaceBar

This chapter discusses the creation of a 3D environment in the popular Autodesk 3D Studio program. After a brief description of the specification, modeling guru Simon Browne shows you how he built an entire world armed with nothing more than a 486/66 and some spectacular modeling and rendering software.

At the end of this chapter there are two smaller sections that provide a brief description of the Grasp code structure that drives The SpaceBar user interface.

Simon built The SpaceBar to provide a fun and nonlinear way to navigate through *Modeling the Dream CD*. In this part of the disc, you enter a room filled with furniture, a dance floor, a cinema, and other places of interest. As you move from one viewing position to another, "hot" items will appear in your window. Selecting one of these hotspots with your mouse will run an animation or trigger a demonstration.

 ## Why We Created The SpaceBar

Our purpose in devising The SpaceBar was two-fold. First, we wanted to create something really special that was interesting to behold and fun to use. Second, we thought you would be interested in reading about how we created it. After trying out several settings for the 3D interface, we settled on Mitchell Waite's original idea for a bar motif, mostly because it presented such an abundance of ideas for links to other pieces of computer artwork.

A screen shot of The SpaceBar is shown in Figure 4-1. It seemed a waste of an opportunity to recreate a bar that already existed, so we settled on a bar set in outer space. This not only

Figure 4-1 The SpaceBar is an interactive 3D environment created by Simon Browne in Autodesk 3D Studio

provided a high-tech atmosphere, but also the scope to try out lots of interesting tricks. As space-weary travelers would not regard a bar full of gleaming aluminum and synthetic plastics as sufficiently different from the functional interiors of their ships, we went for a traditional decor borrowing heavily from the Victorian period. We even made allowances for beings other than humans by providing a "non-oxygen atmosphere room." This room is where you should look for the very weirdest material we have to offer.

The SpaceBar is one huge 3D Studio file containing over 174,000 little triangles known as *faces* that require a machine with 32MB of RAM to render. The actual project file is over 4.5MB in size, has 36 light sources and 56 different materials or surface definitions. Who would be crazy enough to build such a place? Meet Simon Browne.

Simon started working with computers in an ink factory back in 1987, developing experimental systems to drive equipment on the shop floor. At present he runs a service bureau that constantly churns out graphics for rock videos, corporate advertisement, and even furniture design using Autodesk 3D Studio. His extensive experience with these tools made him the perfect person to write the backbone of this chapter.

 What Is Autodesk 3D Studio?

3D Studio (or 3DS as it will be referred to in this chapter), is a self-contained modeling and rendering package currently in its third revision. Figure 4-2 shows what a truly gifted artist such as Rob Stein, the lead animator behind the blockbuster 7th Guest titles can do with it. Although primarily designed for professional video production, 3DS is also a great package for producing 3D animations for multimedia productions. As a high-end product, it rivals the scope and versatility of systems costing ten times as much. Most important, as a PC-based

Figure 4-2 This image by Robert Stein III has been adopted as the unofficial 3DS version 3.0 logo

product, it can take advantage of the ever-cheaper processing power available for this platform. The program is so advanced that it can even distribute the rendering of various frames of an animation sequence across multiple networked machines. But how does it work?

All Objects Are Composed of Faces

Much as a circle may consist of a large number of small straight lines, a sphere or curved surface can be constructed from a large number of flat triangular faces. The more faces that are used, the smoother the resulting surface. To keep track of the location of each of these faces, an x,y,z Cartesian coordinate system can be used. The mathematics required to keep track of a large number of faces could be quite complicated, but with 3DS that's something you don't need to worry about. This program takes away all the pain of having to programmatically define objects in 3D space by providing a responsive interface that handles faces as graphical representations. (If you actually want to define objects in 3D space manually, see the sidebar for some recommendations.)

A face also contains information about its appearance. In addition to describing the color of a face, 3DS also holds information about which surface textures it references at rendering time. If the material in question uses a bitmap file, then the face also must have information as to which part of the bitmap it uses. Finally, each face has a *surface normal* direction.

> If you prefer defining objects using numbers or can't afford the hefty $2700 price tag (at the time of this printing) of 3DS, try out some of the many other modeling packages available from Waite Group Press. *Making Movies on Your PC, Ray Tracing Worlds with POV-Ray, 3D Modeling Lab,* and *Animation How To CD* give step-by-step instructions on how to use some of the most powerful freeware rendering programs on the planet.

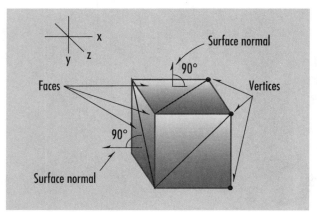

Figure 4-3 A surface normal is an imaginary line that emanates from each face at its center and is perpendicular to its plane

A surface normal is an imaginary line that emanates from each face at its center and is perpendicular to its plane, as shown in Figure 4-3. When 3DS builds an object, the surface normals for each face are pointed outward. This way, when an image is rendered, any face with a surface normal pointed away from the viewpoint can be discarded, vastly simplifying the rendering process.

Cameras

Cameras in 3DS are your window on the world, a point of view on the 3D scene. Creating one is just a matter of choosing two points: the location and the target. You can easily move, turn, or change the perspective of cameras, and you can have many of them in a scene. This feature makes it a snap to create images of an object from several views simultaneously.

Lights

There are three types of lights in 3DS: ambient, omni-directional, and spotlight. Each of these have their own properties which need to be considered when you are designing a scene. Figure 4-4 shows a sphere lit with these three types of light so that you can see the different effects:

 Ambient light is set globally for an entire scene and affects the color of every face. This type of light doesn't originate from any particular place. Instead, it washes over everything, sometimes making it difficult to perceive outlines.

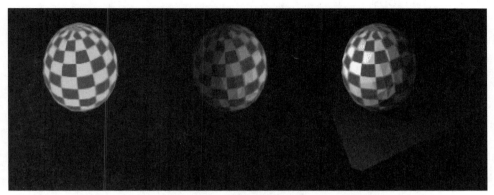

Figure 4-4 This figure shows the effect of lights: ambient, omni-directional, and spotlight

 Omni-directional lights are light sources that emanate from a particular point in space. While they are not capable of casting shadows, they can be set to dim over a predefined distance, just like a natural light.

 Spotlights provide the most realistic lighting for a 3D scene. In their simplest mode, they mimic the behavior of a theater spotlight, allowing precise adjustment of the size of the lit area, known as a *hotspot*, as well as the crispness of the edge where the light decays, known as *falloff*. Spotlights can also reference bitmaps or flics to provide animated illumination, similar to the effect of holding a piece of colored film in front of a flashlight. A large number of spotlights can consume significant system resources, so generally it's wise to use just a few of them and fill in where necessary with weak omni-directional lights.

In the absence of omni-directional lights and spotlights, 3DS projects the ambient color of the scene onto the image plane, which isn't enough to create a realistic image. To fool the eye into seeing depth, more visual clues are needed. These are created by positioning light sources so that they illuminate highlights and cast shadows. To work out the color value of a particular face, the renderer has to combine the effect of these various light sources with the material properties of the face.

Rendering

All we have so far is a database of 3D faces, lights, and a camera. Rendering is the part of the program that crushes all this data down to a bitmap that hopefully portrays what we initially had in mind. This complex series of calculations is carried out automatically with no input from the operator, which is a good thing, because it can sometimes take hours to produce a single frame. If the system is rendering an animation, it might be working flat out for days, so it is of vital importance to have a stable computer.

The Five Components of 3D Studio

How does one take an idea from one's brain and transfer it to the silicon mind of your average 486? Well, it's like a cross between making a plastic model kit and programming. The interface on a computer is still strictly 2D, so you have to build the objects in stages starting from 2D shapes. Let's take a look at the five areas of 3DS that help you build a world and see how they all fit together.

2D Shaper

Before you can create a 3D object, you first have to define it by drawing lines the same way an engineer might produce plans on a drawing board. The 2D Shaper shown in Figure 4-5 is the part of the 3DS program that lets you work with these flat representations, preparing them to be "lofted" into 3D objects.

3D Lofter

3DS has sophisticated 3D modeling capabilities, enabling it to produce complex doubly-curved surfaces. The Lofter works by dragging a 2D shape or cross-section along a 3D path. For example, lofting a circle along a linear path would create a cylinder. If the lofting path were circular, the resulting object would be donut-shaped. As you can see from Figure 4-6, if the circle is lofted along a helical path, a spring results.

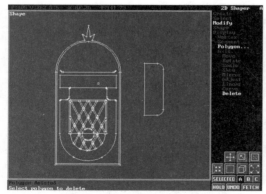

Figure 4-5 The 2D Shaper module is used to create flat shapes from which 3D objects can be constructed

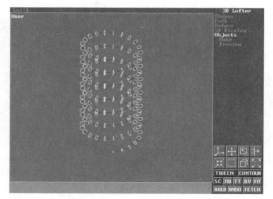

Figure 4-6 The 3D Lofter creates objects by dragging cross-sections created in the 2D Shaper along a path through 3D space

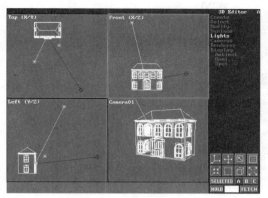

Figure 4-7 The 3D Editor showing top, left, front, and camera views

3D Editor

The core of 3DS is the 3D Editor. Within this module, you prepare a scene for rendering by manipulating entities, creating lights and cameras, and applying materials. Objects can be grouped so that they become elements of a new object. Existing objects can be "machined to fit" by bending or tapering them. It is even possible to subtract one object from another in what is called a *boolean operation.* For example, if you wanted to make a block of Swiss cheese, you would first make the block and then make the holes. A single operation subtracts the holes from the block.

The model is represented in four viewports as in Figure 4-7, conventionally showing top, left, side, and the view from the position of the camera. You can easily change the number of viewports or their orientation. For example, if you were creating an object that is much wider than it is high, such as a car, you might want to have only two viewports, each the entire width of the screen, for representing the side and top views.

Keyframer

The old way of creating an animation was to draw each frame from scratch. 3DS makes it easier. All you have to do is create a series of *keyframes* describing the positions and attributes of objects at specific points, and 3DS "magically" fills in the frames in between. You can think of a keyframe as a point in the animation where a particular event happens, such as a camera reaching a certain position or a light exceeding a specific intensity.

It is also necessary to define how an object approaches and leaves a keyframe. For instance, a bouncing ball requires a keyframe at the apex of its flight and when it hits the ground. At the apex, the ball must pass smoothly through the keyframe, whereas when it hits the ground it must change direction very quickly. Adjusting the acceleration of objects into and out of keyframes is a snap.

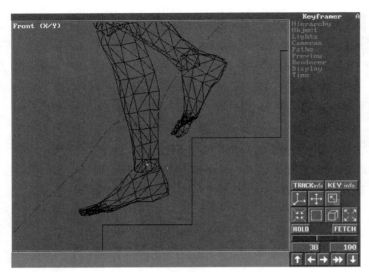

Figure 4-8 The Keyframer showing the path
of a mannequin's ankle

The Keyframer interface is virtually identical to the 3D Editor, but has the added element of time. There is a slider bar at the bottom of the screen that lets you move to a specific frame. In Figure 4-8, you can see a series of icons at the bottom right of the screen for playing back the animation in an unrendered preview mode. It is also possible to show the path of any particular object throughout the animation, which is useful to ensure that objects do not pass through each other unexpectedly.

Materials Editor

The fifth module within 3DS, the Materials Editor, controls the appearance of surfaces by allowing the adjustment of color, roughness, reflectivity, and transparency. A 3DS material in its simplest form has three different color settings that affect the appearance of the object under different lighting conditions. The *ambient* setting determines the color of the object when it is not directly lit, *diffuse* describes the color when illuminated, and *specular* defines the shiny reflective spot.

3DS offers a great deal of flexibility in dealing with the way that objects reflect other objects. Instead of requiring that a reflection be calculated based on the surrounding scene, a picture can be assigned as the reflected image. An image used in this way is called a *reflection map*. Reflection maps can greatly reduce the computer's workload. To produce an accurate reflection showing the surrounding objects in a scene, you can use a *cubic* reflection map. This feature triggers a secondary rendering from all six sides of the object, producing pictures that are then used as reflection maps. Rendering scenes with multiple objects that have been assigned large cubic reflection maps radically increases the amount of computation time required.

Clever use of *opacity mapping* can radically reduce the amount of modeling time required. For example, Figure 4-9 shows two balls. The one on the left shows the effect of opacity mapping, which causes darker areas to be increasingly transparent. This effect is used to create the moving sculpture in the non-oxygen room, which can be seen in Figure 4-10. Even the closest examination of this flic reveals no hint that the underlying 3D geometry is surprisingly simple. The steps around the mobius spiral are created by the application of an animated opacity map rather than by intricate modeling of the spiral itself.

The second ball in Figure 4-9 shows the effect of *bump mapping*. Changes between light and dark areas on the reference bitmap produce the realistic appearance of bumps or ridges on the rendered sphere. Bump mapping works by changing the values of surface normals at specific points on a surface, thereby affecting the calculations involving incident and reflected light. The pitted sections of the doors in The SpaceBar appear to have a rough texture. If this had been modeled with 3D faces instead of bump mapping, it would have taken a lifetime to create, and would have used up vast amounts of memory. The only drawback to using bump maps is that the observer will not see the texture effect when looking tangentially to a surface, but will instead see a smooth silhouette.

Pictures (bitmaps) may be assigned as texture, opacity, or bump maps, so let's look at each of these in turn. The most basic way of using a bitmap is to apply it to the surface of an object as a texture map. For example, you could apply a scanned image of a wooden texture to create a wooden object. This points out the dilemma of trying to create 3D objects using 2D textures. The simple case of a tabletop gives us little trouble; the bitmap can be applied parallel to the top edge in a repeated or "tiled" manner. In the case of a curved object, however, the bitmap has to be wrapped around the object using either a cylindrical or spherical mapping attribute. It is worth noting that through 3DS' IPAS interface, it is possible to have 3D texture maps that are generated algorithmically to produce swirling smoke or true wood grains.

Figure 4-9 The ball on the left shows opacity mapping while the ball on the right shows bump mapping

Figure 4-10 Clever use of opacity mapping, such as in the non-oxygen room, can radically reduce the amount of time needed to model 3D objects

Figure 4-11 The SpaceBar's jukebox is a great metaphor, providing a natural menu to various sound bites and General MIDI tracks

Building the Jukebox

For a closer look at 3DS, let's examine the construction of a 1950s-style jukebox. Since much of the material on the CD is audible, a metaphor was required that would provide an intuitive interface to sound, and what could be better than a jukebox? The one we settled on, in Figure 4-11, is a design classic. The wonderful swooping curves and rich selection of interesting materials make it ideal for our study. It also presents an opportunity for a small animation: a compact disc being moved from the rack onto the platter. LPs? We can't have anything as low-tech as vinyl for The SpaceBar.

Building Cross-Sections in the 2D Shaper

The key to a smooth modeling session in 3DS is to produce an organized and accurate set of drawings. Although Simon could have produced everything in 3DS, he used AutoCAD to produce the plan views. With its comprehensive set of utilities, AutoCAD can be faster for building an accurate set of shapes than 3DS. These shapes were then pulled in via the drawing interchange format (.DXF).

Lofting the Pieces

The jukebox was built from six basic elements: the main wooden cabinet, the panels, the speaker grill, the glass bubble, the swoopy double-curved surround, and the trim. The wooden cabinet is a straightforward loft; the shape is the same at both ends of the lofting path and its depth is the overall depth of the object. By using the main shape of the cabinet with the cut-out nested, the Lofter will recognize this as a hole and only place faces pointing outward away from the object. A wood texture was mapped parallel to the front of the cabinet. Since the rear of the jukebox is not seen, these faces were deleted to reduce the complexity of the model and save memory. Even if faces are never seen, they still take up memory and increase the amount of time it takes to redraw the scene as the viewpoint changes. The more faces you have, the more memory is required and the harder a model is to work with.

The panels and speaker grill are lofted like the cabinet, but they are much thinner. The resulting object was then autosmoothed in the 3D Editor to give the impression of rounded edges. This facility miraculously creates the illusion of smooth surfaces without the need for many faces by averaging the direction of the surface normals on the object at rendering time.

As you can see in Figure 4-12, the glass bubble was scaled as it was lofted to produce this round exterior. The glass material used is completely transparent, but has a reflection map made up of small camera shots of the scene. Hence, the bubble appears to actually reflect the environment. Using cubic reflection maps in this way provides a much quicker alternative to completely ray-tracing the scene. If the reflections on surfaces appear to reflect the color and some of the form of their environment, the brain accepts this as a viable image clue and makes the necessary mental leap, perceiving it as an accurate reflection. The same cubic reflection map is used throughout the scene in different places and on different materials. The actual map was shot from the bar, which means that objects on the periphery appear to reflect the center of the room.

The metallic band around the middle of the jukebox was the most difficult element to create. As you can see in Figure 4-13, it uses a shape lofted along a curved path that exactly

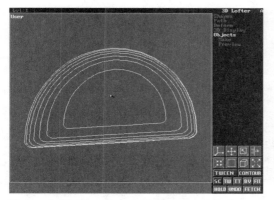

Figure 4-12 The glass bubble was scaled as it was lofted to produce a smooth, rounded exterior

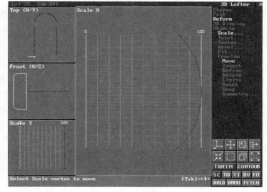

Figure 4-13 The middle band was created by lofting a shape around a curved path following the outline of the cabinet

follows the outline of the cabinet. This way, as the cross-section or 2D shape is dragged around the lofting path, it places this metallic band exactly around the periphery of the cabinet. As the shape moves around the path, it is scaled in only one dimension so as to flair out to its widest point at the front of the cabinet.

Creation and Application of Materials

Five different materials have been applied to the various parts of the jukebox. Some of these are created using IPAS routines. IPAS is an interface through which external programs can be slotted into 3DS to extend its capabilities. For example, one group of IPAS routines known as PXPs will create new geometric shapes based on existing ones. With these you can apply the swimming motion of a manta ray or the effect of rippling water to almost any object. Another group of IPAS routines called IXPs applies image-processing effects to images immediately after they have been rendered but before they have been written to disk. These programs give the animator the ability to manipulate images in a variety of ways such as by adding realistic lens flares to enhance the lighting of their scene. AXPs are animated stand-in processes that generate 3D geometry at rendering time. For example, using the cyclone generator you could draw a cube and assign it to be a cyclone composed of 1,000 particles. The cyclone generator also lets you control the inner and outer rotation speeds as well as introducing a degree of chaos to give your animation a natural look. The family of IPAS routines that we are most interested in here, however, are known as SXPs, which generate true 3D materials such as the wood grain described previously in the mapping section.

Here is a brief description of each material:

Smoky glass This surface is actually not bitmapped, but is derived from a fractal smoke algorithm implemented as an IPAS external process. This smoke IPAS is used here as a texture and opacity map, and can be animated to produce a swirling effect. The same reflection map used for the bubble's glass texture gives the impression of high gloss.

Frosted glass This texture is scanned from a photo of a frosted glass shower door. The resulting bitmap is used both as a texture and as a bump map.

Wood grain The wood texture took a whole day to get right. Natural wood scatters light in a non-uniform way that makes it appear to have depth, and of course no two pieces look quite the same. The best way to begin creating a wood material is to start with a scanned image of actual wood, but this on its own produces a flat-looking grain with no variation. Therefore, the contrast of the original wood image was increased and used as a shininess map. The varying levels of reflectiveness over the surface of the wood are what makes the texture so rich. Another benefit to this approach is that no two sections of the wood will look exactly the same; the varying shininess of the wood grain will interact differently with the different lighting in various parts of the room.

To conserve memory, the wood grain on the base of the jukebox is the same as on the wall panels and on the surface of the bar. As each texture used in this scene takes up at least 400K of memory, the number of different textures in the whole model needed to be kept to a minimum.

Chrome The jukebox has chrome trim along the sides. The resulting elements were smoothed along their width but not along their length to produce a ridged effect. The chrome is the same chrome as used in the rest of the scene. It is created using a metallic rendering algorithm that provides a great deal of reflection blur.

Two-sided chrome 3DS uses a rather clever mechanism to discard faces that are not needed at rendering time. As you have already seen, each face has a surface normal that usually points away from the object. By discarding faces with surface normals pointing away from the camera, 3DS eliminates roughly half the model, greatly increasing rendering efficiency. If an object needs to be visible from both sides (like the CDs in the jukebox), a two-sided material forces the renderer to consider both sides when computing the picture. Transparent materials are commonly two-sided, since we need to see the inside through the outside.

Constructing the Ceiling

Simon created the vaulted ceiling of The SpaceBar first because it defines the character of the room and provides the overall dimensions of the scene. First, a single section was lofted, as Figure 4-14 shows. Notice that this object has been scaled and flattened to produce a gently changing surface. The object was then rotated and copied to form a 10x10 matrix of sections constituting the entire roof. In other words, the ceiling is composed of 100 sections built from the loft in Figure 4-14. Adjacent sections are all welded together so that any vertices within a certain distance of each other are amalgamated into one in such a way as to preserve

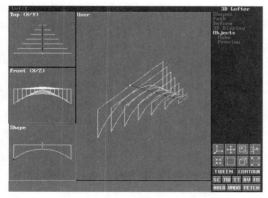

Figure 4-14 The loft of the single ceiling section, which is then copied; the copies are then joined together

any faces that those vertices may define. This not only prevents any gaps in the structure, but also reduces the number of vertices in the model.

The stone texture was assigned to all 100 units of the ceiling in one operation. First, Simon manually entered the exact dimensions for the area over which the surface was to be mapped. In 3DS parlance, this is known as defining the *region fit*. The texture map was then set to tile in a 10x10 matrix when applied. This technique assures that each map unit exactly fits over the roof joins, thereby disguising the overly precise construction. As a result, the ceiling looks rough, rather than having straight lines between its tiles. To have done the region fit and applied the map on a single unit and then replicated the unit 100 times would have amplified any error tremendously. It also would have left straight lines between the sections clearly visible.

Finally, a central section was cut out by deleting all the vertices within an area and a new, simpler section was slotted into its place. The smooth surface applied to the ceiling over this central area enhances the impression of volume.

The exterior wall was constructed next. Because the plexiglass window needed to reflect the scene in the bar as well as show the stars outside, Simon created an auto-reflecting transparent material for the glass. He did this by placing a second camera in the scene in the mirror position to our viewing camera. The resulting image is then flipped and matted into the final image automatically, easily creating a stunning effect.

Creating the View Outside Using Video Post

Although any worthwhile space scene needs an abundance of nebulae, spaceships, and extraterrestrial paraphernalia, the basis has to be lots of different stars. 3DS comes with a routine that creates great starfields from scratch. This routine works through a submodule of the Keyframer called the Video Post Processor, or *Video Post* for short. This module modifies or creates pictures in layers, like building up a picture with images drawn onto clear film in traditional cel animation. It will also coordinate these layers over a series of frames. This very powerful feature gives the PC capabilities which, while slower than dedicated machines, delivers an end-product just as good. It is important to understand that in their most elementary form, these layers are simply a composite of the constituent images. The real power of Video Post comes in calling IPAS routines to manipulate the layered image algorithmically.

The layout of the Video Post compositor, shown in Figure 4-15 shows that three image-processing IPAS routines are in the queue to be run on the rendered image. The details of what these routines do is listed below:

 STARS.IXP takes the current camera position and a data file containing star positions and produces a starfield. Because the starfield production is linked to the camera angle, the starfield appears to move when the camera does, giving a perfect backdrop. The first time this routine is called in the Video Post queue, it generates only a few stars.

GLOW.IXP takes the stars made in the previous stage and blurs any pixels that are above a given luminance value, making them look like bright light sources.

 STARS.IXP is now called a second time, with a much more populated database, to fill in the gaps between the glowing stars.

 KFSCENE is the geometry of the scene as viewed from the camera. Video Post blends this over the other layers to provide the final result, shown in Figure 4-16.

Creation of Planet Texture

The planet texture is a combination of a bitmap of earth and a custom-drawn map of planet "lights." The map of the earth is used as a texture and bump map, giving the color and corresponding ridges of the planet. The lights are created by using a second bitmap applied with a self-illumination property so that it will be visible on the dark portions of the planet.

Creation of the Nebula Using Fractal Software

Many shareware fractal-creation programs can provide a beautiful random image to be used for something like the nebula. We feel the best two are Fractint and WinFract, which can be found in the Waite Group Press guides *Fractal Creations Second Edition* and *Fractals for Windows: Hands-on Fractal Exploration.*

The particular nebula pattern in Figure 4-16 is generated from Yorke-type mathematics and rendered to a .GIF file, which is then mapped as a texture and opacity map. We use an opacity map so that the areas of the fractal that would otherwise be black are transparent, allowing the stars behind the nebula to show through.

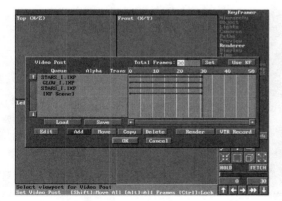

Figure 4-15 The Video Post module of 3DS builds up pictures over layers on top of the rendered image

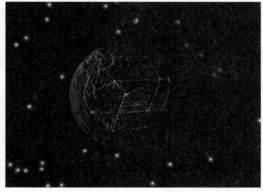

Figure 4-16 The final starfield image, composited with Video Post

Other Objects in The SpaceBar

The following pages provide some general information regarding how certain other objects and animations were created. The lava lamp, mushroom cloud, and morphing monitors are in The SpaceBar lounge; the green fog and mercury fountain can be found in the non-oxygen room.

Lava Lamp and Mushroom Cloud

The lava lamp and the mushroom cloud are very similar, in that they simulate the appearance of fluids in motion. While there are routines that can simulate still bodies of fluid (such as the one used in the fountain in the non-oxygen atmosphere room), generally the way that blobs of fluid separate and reform ceaselessly in a lava lamp is at odds with a meshed-geometry approach to computer modeling. Therefore, an artistic compromise must be made between what is possible and what looks good enough.

Both the lamp and the cloud were created using many small balls that continuously rotate and move around in such close proximity as to be indistinguishable from each other. The balls that form the mushroom cloud are formed into groups of six, which rotate inward and are controlled hierarchically from a central dummy object. This dummy object is then copied and rotated and linked to another dummy object. The final dummy object is then scaled and moved over time to produce the impression of the cloud growing as it rises. Figure 4-17 shows a screen shot of the cloud from the Keyframer. The final touch is to map an animation of real fire onto the spheres.

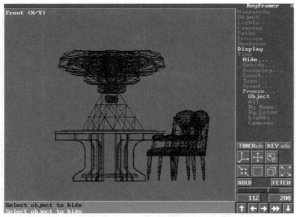

Figure 4-17 The illusion of fluids is created by using many small, hierarchically linked balls that rotate in close proximity to each other

48

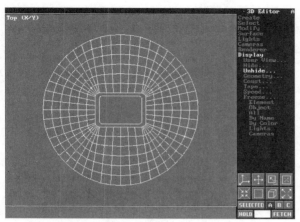

Figure 4-18 The tabletop intermediate morph object, as seen in the 3D Editor

Morphing a Monitor from a Tabletop

As any computer-graphics buff knows, *morphing* is a process in which one object seamlessly changes into another. It is commonly used in the media to produce a strong association between objects. The SpaceBar has a fairly simple example of this process, involving a flat sheet stretching to produce a TV screen while leaving the tabletop on which it appears undisturbed. 3DS has the ability to perform morphs, but not with a straightforward command. Both the initial and target objects must have the same number of vertices. Also, the corresponding faces on each object must be joined in the same order. The simplest way of going about this is to create one object and then edit it to produce the second. The TV-screen morph was achieved by creating an intermediate object between the two and performing two morphs instead of one.

As you can see in Figure 4-18, the initial tabletop is a loft between the screen shape and the circle that is the edge of the table. This initial flat object was created by scaling the lofted object to .01 percent of its thickness, at which point it appears to be totally flat. The final tabletop has the vertices that comprise the screen pulled and tilted in the direction of the camera.

Non-Oxygen Room

The creation of the non-oxygen room was the most fun of all. The overall greenness of the gas and decor is a change from the warm tones of The SpaceBar. The room is sparsely filled with alien artifacts and has seats that no human backside would be comfortable in.

Green Fog

The green fog is produced by a combination of two effects. 3DS has homogeneous fog built into the renderer that merely obscures distant objects by reducing their contrast. The second

Figure 4-19 The mercury fountain uses two IPAS external processes to create the spray and undulating fluid effects

fog effect takes place on a plane about two feet off the floor. This fog actually uses the same animated smoke pattern as used on the bubble of the jukebox, but tinted green. The roof here has also been assigned a proportion of this texture.

Mercury Fountain

The mercury fountain shown in Figure 4-19 is no great modeling feat. It uses two IPAS external processes to create its magic. The first routine is a procedural texture map that simulates ripples when used as a bump map. As you can see from the liquid in the base of the fountain, this technique is great for creating the effect of a pool of "mercury" when used in conjunction with a cubic reflection map. The second routine uses what is known as *animated standin process* to algorithmically generate geometry at rendering time. All you would see in the 3D Editor would be a big box over the area where the spray appears in the rendered flic. The calculations to handle gravity are built in automatically, making this routine a snap to use. Surface properties for the individual balls are defined by whatever material is assigned to the cube (which in this case is chrome).

Grasp 5.0 as the Authoring System

Just having a bunch of pretty pictures and fancy animations doesn't make an interactive interface. To start with, you need to lay out an attractive screen design that has buttons on it for triggering interactivity. On the coding side, you need to build a structure for monitoring the mouse so you can respond to the user's requests. Although we've given a great deal of coverage to the Grasp development system in Chapter 3 regarding its abilities to work with sounds and flics, very little was mentioned about dealing with user responses. The remainder of this chapter looks at Grasp's interactive capabilities and generally describes how the interface works.

Responding to Mouse Movements

As you can see from the map in Figure 4-20, there are eight vantage points from which you can look in any of eight directions within The SpaceBar. Of these 64 different views, many have no hotspots that can be selected with your mouse. If, when changing your position or view, you come across a screen that does have a "hot" icon, this fact is noted in the status line where you can read a description of the interactive option available.

Whenever a view or position changes, Grasp searches a data table for events that need to be available at that particular position and view. If it finds the current position and view in the table, the Grasp IFMOUSE command is set to trigger an action whenever the mouse button is depressed over a region of the screen specified in the table. Table 4-1 is a short sample of what the data table looks like so you can get a feel for the information it contains. The first three columns are self-explanatory. The next four define the size of the hot region in pixels, with 0,0 (X1=0, Y1=0) being the lower left corner of the screen.

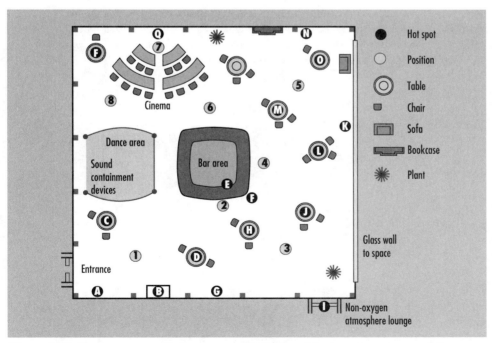

Figure 4-20 Users can move between any of eight positions scattered around the room

Position	View	Description	X1	Y1	X2	Y2	Label
1	1	Killer Chess II by Mike Mulholland	10	10	20	20	CHESS
1	1	Waite Group Spring '94 Catalog	30	60	40	80	SPRING
1	2	Chernobyl Encasement Proposal	20	40	10	80	CHERN

Table 4-1 A sample of The SpaceBar data table

Program flow is as follows:

1. Initialization occurs, defaulting to view 1 and position 1.

2. A subroutine is then run which processes the data table. In the case of Table 4-1, two hot regions would be found because there are two hot spots listed in the table for view 1, position 1.

3. The status line is updated to hold the information in the two description fields and the main loop is set to detect mouse depressions that occur within the two areas 10,10,20,20 and 30,60,40,80 using the Grasp IFMOUSE command.

4. Should one of these IFMOUSE conditions return true because the user has selected a hot area, program control is passed to the part of the Grasp program containing the label in the Action column.

Certain demos use so much memory and machine resources that a complete shutdown of Grasp is required. To run one of these demos, a batch file is written out and executed by DOS based upon the value of the ERRORLEVEL that Grasp returns when it terminates. This is exactly how the MTD interface works.

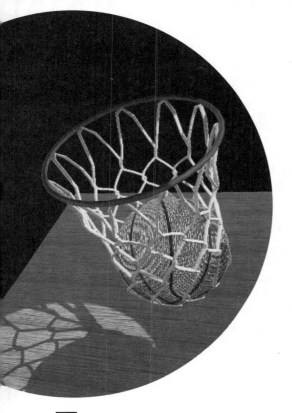

CHAPTER 5
3D ANIMATIONS

This chapter introduces you to some real power users of 3D Studio. They range from an 18-year-old student just embarking on his formal education to old-timers reliving the creative days of their youth. Autodesk 3D Studio has established itself as the tool of choice among today's PC-based 3D artists because of its power and ease of use. While there are certainly less expensive packages available, 3D Studio seems to be the tool everyone wants to use. The second section of this chapter relates the experience of artists using ray tracing programs such as POV-Ray and Polyray. Wherever possible, the source code for these 3D animations has been included on the CD in the directory of the artist responsible.

While some of these works of art may be the efforts of many people, the individual contributions have been listed under the name of the person who signed the demos over to us for publication. If it is clear that a particular demo is the result of a group effort, we have been careful to point that out to you.

All contributors filled in a questionnaire describing their work and the techniques that they use. In general, the length of their sections in the text reflects the amount of pertinent information that they provided. Along with the questions that you might expect us to ask such as those relating to particular tools, we asked all of the contributors to share with us their vision of the future of computer-based artistic expression. We hope you enjoy their varied and somewhat unusual responses.

Animations Created with Autodesk 3D Studio

In this section, as well as in the following section on ray-traced animations, we introduce artists in alphabetical order by last name. We also provide their company name, their home town and country of residence, the path of the animations on the CD, and the size of the animations.

Paths and Files The files that comprise these animations can all be found in subdirectories off of the \FLICS directory on the CD. In those cases where the animations consist of several different files, DOS wildcards have been used. For example \FARMER*.FLI designates all files with the extension .FLI located in the \FLICS\FARMER subdirectory. For more information on the structure of the CD, see Chapter 2.

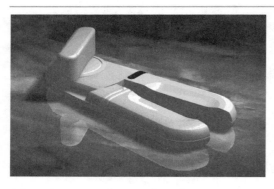

Adrian Dodds

Adrian Dodds Design Service
Bicester, Oxfordshire, UK
\DODDS\CULINARE.FLC   2.1MB

Figure 5-1 The Culinaire can opener

Adrian designs products and produces animations for a living, creating presentations used for marketing applications at trade shows and exhibitions. He believes that this area of computer-based presentation is destined to become an essential part of new product development. The Culinaire animation shown in Figure 5-1 was part of a marketing presentation.

The limited range of colors in CULINARE is the major reason why it looks so photorealistic. As you can see when you view this sequence, the color scheme is dominated by a range from cream through to red, and the general level of saturation (intensity of the color) is quite subdued. When an animation includes wide ranges of colors from several parts of the spectrum, the images often take on a rough and contoured appearance as the differences between each of the 256 colors become discernible to the eye. If you were to load CULINARE into Animator Pro and sort the palette by spectrums, you would see a continuous gradation, with each color being only slightly different from the adjacent one. In contrast, doing the same with Mulholland's Hellfire animation would result in a raucous party of color with representatives from all bands of the spectrum invited.

Merlin Farmer

Crystal Cave Computers
Cartersville, IL, USA
\FARMER*.FLI   31.1MB

Figure 5-2 A shot from CWING.FLI, an animation of the Crystal Cave logo

Merlin describes himself as a former starving poet, musician, and artist who mistakenly gave up the good life in order to maintain steady employment. When he started Crystal Cave, he focused on computer and electronics design consulting, but increasingly over the past year and a half he has been developing multimedia applications. Through multimedia, Merlin feels he has found a path back to the days of his artistic youth in the 1970s.

Recently, Crystal Cave made the jump to professional video production. To date, they have produced two TV commercials, a rock video, and an industrial video. For production, they use a Sony SVO Pro SVHS deck and a Hi8 camcorder. Merlin and his associates are convinced that the trend is toward many more multimedia applications being produced in home offices as production and video directing comes increasingly from sole proprietors. While not a full-blown service bureau, Crystal Cave is more than willing to help transfer the graphics of other artists to videotape.

Creating the Crystal Cave Logo

The Crystal Cave Computers logo in Figure 5-2 started out on paper as a letterhead before being produced as a 2D animation using Tempra Turbo Animator. The jump to 3D Studio required a complete redesign. The sphere in this flic represents a crystal ball that they use to keep an eye on emerging technology. The pilot's wings represent experience and qualifications. Merlin is particularly pleased with the material he created for the crystal ball. He points out that it is not too transparent or overly reflective. The idea was to capture a certain amount of weight and density while retaining the transparency of crystal.

SPACE.FLI

The Spacecraft flic is 15MB in size. The different camera angles used in this animation were composited together with the Video Post features of 3D Studio. The ship is a simple dumbbell structure created from two identical shapes created in the 2D Shaper, then lofted using the Fit tool with symmetry turned on. With the Fit tool, you can build complex objects very quickly by defining horizontal and vertical cross-sections. The windows and four engines were added in the 3D Editor, the engines having been lifted from an aircraft mesh that came with 3D Studio Release 3.0 World Creating Toolkit CD.

Figure 5-3 Diamonds uses a variety of IPAS effects to enhance the reflectiveness of the objects in the scene

DIAMONDS.FLI

The Diamonds flic is part of a commercial for a dance club. The first diamond was created by taking a simple sphere and pulling vertices into the right positions. Although the material used is a little too transparent for a still image, like the one in Figure 5-3, it works well with the highlight filter in a moving animation. To get the right effect, Merlin turned off the hue option of the highlight filter. Rendering the flic at 320x200 resolution took only three hours, but the video version at 512x484 required over 21 hours of computing time to complete.

Tom Guthery

FLIX Productions
DelValle, TX, USA
\GUTHERY\STARSHIP.FLI   3.1MB

Figure 5-4 A frame from STARSHIP.FLI

Starship Nightshift is a 732-frame flic Tom created for fun while taking a break from his usual work creating children's software and corporate multimedia applications. The quality of this piece reveals Tom's experience in the area of professional animation. He started working on films nearly 20 years ago. Most of his early work was on what he calls "personal films" that were partially underwritten by three grants from the National Endowment for Arts. Tom feels that his film experience is strongly reflected in what he does on the PC. Rather than rely on computer modeling programs, he uses more traditional techniques. Generally, he grabs sequences of video using the ComputerEyes RT capture card and then manipulates them with Animator Pro.

Tom used Animator Pro to paint the background for the space scene in Starship Nightshift, shown in Figure 5-4. The dust clouds were achieved using the Airbrush tool's jumble and smoothing inks. The stars, clouds, and planets were each created as separate layers and then composited together, similar to what Tom used to do when he painted backgrounds for cel animations using watercolors and an airbrush. As he points out, however, in traditional animations, if you mess up a cel you have to start over again. With the PC, you can always save your stages and only discard the ones you won't need.

The logo was created using Animator Pro's optics effects, but the multicolored fonts came from Deluxe Paint II Enhanced. All of the paint programs for the PC have their strengths and weaknesses, so Tom just chooses the parts of each that he thinks are best. For example, he drew the outline of the starship using Pictor (the paint program that comes with Grasp) because it is easy to use and he is very familiar with it. He added the colors later with Animator Pro.

The "Cloud Tank" Effect

Adding organic elements to a PC animation always creates a more realistic feel. In this animation, the swirling clouds were produced using a "cloud-tank" effect similar to the technique used in the film *Close Encounters of the Third Kind:* They filled a large tank with water and then recorded the effect of adding various other liquids to it while agitating the mixture. When these sequences were composited into the film, the result looked natural.

For the little planet in Starship, Tom used only a small jar placed in front of a white card, which reflected the light back to the camera. Food coloring was swirled around with a spoon as the ComputerEyes RT capture card grabbed several full-motion sequences. Tom then used Animator Pro to reverse the colors so that the "clouds" became white and the background black. The result was then composited onto the planet, which had been previously drawn on the background. To give the clouds an appearance of height on the edge of the planet surface, Tom used a circular mask that was slightly larger than the drawn planet. Since the resulting sequence was too short, the beginning and end were dissolved together to form a loop.

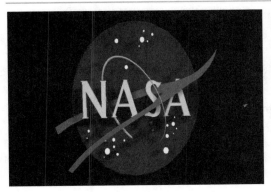

Chris Johnston

NASA Lewis Research Center
Cleveland, OH, USA
\JOHNSTON*.FLC   19.4MB

Figure 5-5 The NASA logo created by Chris Johnston in 3D Studio

Chris creates animations and writes software of all types as part of his job as an engineer with NASA. A chemist by profession, his specialty is nuclear magnetic resonance spectroscopy.

The three animations Chris sent all show a prototype of a progammable multi-zone furnace which has 24 active zones. PMZF3A2.FLC shows off the construction of the complete furnace,

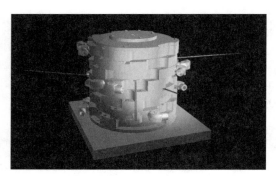

Figure 5-6 The progammable multi-zone furnace prototype from PMZF3A2.FLC

including the 105° rotation between steps and the sample change capability. PMZB.FLC illustrates, using a smaller furnace stack, how easily an entire segment can be removed for servicing. PZ2.FLC shows a single segment in detail, including the internal cooling channel.

The point in all these animations is to graphically demonstrate the characteristics and design features of the furnace both to those within NASA and to the general public. The hope is that once people have seen these visualizations, they will better understand the design and have more faith in the hardware implementation. One unique aspect of this project for Chris is the ability to show people a convincing picture of the furnace design while it is still under development. A few seconds of video help to convey that information much better than any detailed discussion of CAD drawings ever could.

Chris is particularly happy with the reflections on the furnace, as well as the general lighting and transparency. In PMZF3A2.FLC, an image from which is shown in Figure 5-6, a reflection map was used to make the metal look shiny. Chris created this using a Targa card to grab a sequence of 24 images from a 3/4-inch videotape deck. A lot of work went into finding the right aluminum color that would contrast with the insulators and the header coil wires. The effect of transparency was created with the Video Post module of 3D Studio. Two frames were generated, one with a glass material and the other with the aluminum metal, and then Video Post was used to cross-fade between them.

Henry Köhtz

Munich, Germany
\KOHTZ\CAM*.FLI   57MB

Figure 5-7 A frame from the Birdy sequence

The Birdy sequence in Figure 5-7 is one of the most comical pieces that we have to share with you. It is very simple in terms of the number and complexity of objects, yet because the story is so well executed this sequence is a pleasure to watch again and again. Henry explains that to plan and execute a sequence such as Birdy, he divides the project into three stages. Here he describes the elements that went into each.

Planning

First, the entire script for the animation had to be worked out using paper and pencil. The five major areas of planning for this sequence were:

 Placement and movement of the camera and objects

 Speed and acceleration of the camera and other objects in the scene

 Partitioning the screen into different areas

 Determining the length of each scene

 Sketching out previews with simple boxes to gain a rough idea of how the sequence would eventually look

Modeling

The second step involved transferring ideas from the sketches into a 3D Studio model, starting by creating each of the meshes with all of their detail. Before applying maps to the objects, Henry made test renderings to check the motion. Many of the objects were actually only duplicates or instances of other objects copied from "true" geometry in the Keyframer. For example, in the 3D Editor, the chain which hangs from the cuckoo clock is actually very short. Looking at the chain in Keyframer reveals a long object composed of copies of the much smaller object in the 3D Editor. Henry feels that creating Keyframer instances keeps your model size and rendering times down. For example, in the entire 3,200 frames of this sequence, there are over 2,000 key positions, but the entire 3D Studio file is only 600K in size.

Assigning

The majority of the final stage involved the creation of lighting and the assignment of materials. Because the mesh of the bird was relatively static, it was important to have a particularly nice map. The lighting for the scene consists of two omni-directional lights and a single stationary spotlight. The sequence took 100 hours to render on a 486 equipped with 16MB of RAM. Henry reports that timing the final sequences and cutting the camera shots together so that the movements made sense were the most difficult parts of the project.

The most important thing that Henry learned in producing Birdy was the value of approaching the problem after taking a break from it. He found that poring over his project for too long made him lose some of his creativity. Leaving the project allowed Henry to view it in a different light when he resumed, adding numerous refinements that he wouldn't have thought of if he'd worked straight through.

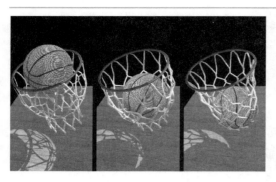

Rick Lapidus

Video Production Marketing
Boca Raton, FL, USA
\LAPIDUS\BALL4.FLC   4.6MB

Figure 5-8 BALL4.FLC demonstrates the morphing of complex shapes; every twelfth frame is shown here

Rick formed the South Florida 3D Studio Users Group primarily to help new users learn more about the tools and get involved with producing animations themselves. He also figured that pooling the experience of a group of people would make it easier to solve the problems that inevitably arise in configuring some of the more specialized pieces of hardware and software needed to do video production with 3D Studio. Since most computer retailers in his area had never heard of, let alone used, products such as frame buffers and video tape controllers, users needed somewhere else to turn.

Rick constructed the mapping for the ball in Animator Pro with the intent of using it as a planar map. After a dozen attempts using various combinations of mapping, tiling, and lofting techniques, Rick tried a different approach. What seemed to work the best was to draw half the ball and let the computer project that same map on the other half. With planar mapping on a sphere, the map tends to warp at the edges, so even though the stripes will always match up, the ball won't look right until properly adjusted. Rick achieved the final result by using a map that compensates for the warping effect. He created the texture map by tiling an orange and red pattern inside a copy of the warped bump map.

Instead of trying to map the net, Rick decided that a complex mesh was needed for the close-ups. He constructed the net around the ball by creating a complex set of 11 elements, each with 768 faces. The ability to see the 3D mesh from within the Lofter and Shaper was a big help in constructing this complex object. Once the first piece was lofted, Rick used the (SHIFT) key to clone the element. These newly created elements were then rotated into an exact position using Angle Snap.

The most challenging part of this animation was creating the morph using the Ripple IPAS routine. The final morph is actually composed of two different sets of ripples. By mixing different amplitudes and periods, Rick was able to get just the effect he wanted. One of the keys was to set the amplitude to be equal to the distance between the ball and the bottom of the net in its stretched position.

Pero Maticevic

MWM Design
London, UK
\MATICEVI*.FL?   44.2MB

Figure 5-9 A frame from
ENTRANCE.FLI

MWM Design was founded in 1992 by Pero Maticevic, Julian Woropay, and Olga Medenica. The company comprises a network of freelance architects, artists, film makers, sculptors, graphic designers, model makers, and engineers, with a wide range of skills. Their specialty is creating videos and computer-generated walkthroughs. Although they use sophisticated tools, a guiding principle of the company is to emphasize expertise and imagination over hardware and fancy tricks. During their first two years they have won the following awards:

 CadDesk 3D Studio Competition 1992: 1st Prize.

 CadDesk AutoCAD Presentation Competition 1992: 1st Prize.

 Water Sculpture Design Competition, Jones of Oswestry 1993: 2nd Prize.

ENTRANCE.FLI

This project was a refurbishment job for a civil engineering firm. The animation shown in Figure 5-9 was part of the design process. An initial animation without textures was first created to help the client confirm the design. After some modifications, ENTRANCE.FLI was rendered as a preview of the proposed changes to the structure.

The Jones of Oswestry Water Sculpture

The water sculpture in Figure 5-10 won Pero second place in a design competition. In his words, "The sculpture represents an equilibrium of forces, but it is an attempt to create a dynamic scene with static elements. Exaggerated stress in the sculpture suggests that movement is possible if the balance is broken. Therefore it is not a frozen moment; it has a future. The steel and water materials have radically different properties yet are treated equally."

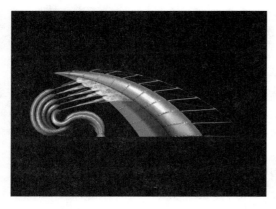

Figure 5-10 The Blade: water sculpture design contest entry

Bruce Meikle

Fire Media
Toronto, Ontario, Canada
\MEIKLE\RADSAT5.FLI   2.1MB

Figure 5-11 A frame from RADSAT5.FLI

The frame in Figure 5-11 is part of an animation of the RADARSAT radar-tracking building designed for the Canadian Space Agency by the Webb Zerafa Menkes Housden Partnership, Architects. The modeling was done in AutoCAD and rendered in 3D Studio to explore possible design directions being considered by the architectural firm. Once the actual modeling was done, Bruce thought it would be a shame not to explore 3D Studio's capabilities and produce an animation.

The team at Fire Media had a lot of fun creating the animated texture map that was used to represent the signals "beamed" into space. The beam is actually present throughout the animation; it's just hidden for the first 60 frames by a completely black section of an animated opacity map. (For more information about animated opacity maps, see the section on the Material Editor in Chapter 4.) To animate the beam, Bruce created a flic of moving streaks that was used as both a texture map and an opacity map. This material was then applied to a cylinder and a cone shape which were both linked to the rotating dish. When using a flic as an opacity map, it is important to keep the length of the map the same as that of the overall flic.

Bruce used both IBM and Macintosh computers for this project. On the IBM side, 3D Studio was the main workhorse. For editing image maps, Bruce used Aldus Photostyler.

Bruce feels that a good deal of computer art has gotten by on its novelty. Trying to keep up with the breakneck pace of changing technology, one runs the risk of being more interested in the equipment than in the final output. More and more, however, Bruce sees the emphasis put on content and quality. The computer is increasingly becoming a tool, not an end in itself.

Michael Mulholland

Student of Computer Animation and Visuals
Bournemouth University
Bournemouth, UK
\FLICS\MULHOLLA*.FLI   117MB

Mike wins the prize for having the largest allocation of disc space on the CD. His three sequences, Killer Chess II, Pinball, and Hellfire total over 116MB in size. At the age of 17, this artist produced Killer Chess, an amazing sequence that is one of the highlights of the first book in this series. Unlike many traditional artists who have moved to the computer, Mike has always been fascinated by this medium. His first machine was the BBC Micro, but he soon moved up to the Atari ST where he experimented with CyberPaint. Perhaps one of the reasons that Mike is so good with 3D Studio is that three of the primary developers of 3D Studio created CyberPaint on the Atari many years ago, when that was the microcomputer of choice for animation.

Presently Mike is completing his first year of a "Computer Animation and Visualization" course at Bournemouth University that features use of the CGAL system running on a HP9700s under Unix version 5 and X-Windows. Each machine has 32MB of RAM and a 1.2Gig hard disk. While the new tools and techniques he is learning are opening up new horizons, he continues to keep a 486/33 in his room so he can continue to work on his own personal projects and commissions.

Pinball

Pinball uses a very simple 3D mesh relying on reflection maps, spotlights, and bitmaps to recreate the visual complexity of a pinball machine. First, Mike used Animator Pro to create a large rectangular bitmap of stars on a black background before applying it to the surface of the pinball machine. A second large bitmap creates the raised score display. The ball is a completely reflective sphere, providing a good demonstration of the reflection mapping capabilities of 3D Studio. Two spotlights, one red and one yellow, are hierarchically linked, with their targets locked on the pinball to create a variety of effects as the colors of the lights mix with the shadows.

The most complex part of this animation was working out the camera flight path. While Mike simply linked the camera target to the pinball, he placed the position of the camera manually every few frames. By spending a great deal of time placing the camera, Mike was able to assure both a good view of the ball and a smooth camera path. Because 3D Studio lets you see

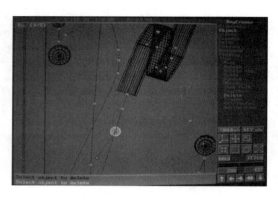

Figure 5-12 3D Studio allows the user to toggle the visibility of the path of an object on and off, facilitating not only exact placement, but also control over the rate of acceleration

the path of an object's movements thoughout an animation, as Figure 5-12 shows, Mike could precisely position the camera on the ball while still allowing for graceful changes in direction.

The entire animation did not take long; the majority of the modeling was done in a single weekend. After discarding several ideas, the final renderings and corrections were finished in a total of two weeks. Mike created this animation on a 386/33 with only 4 megs of memory and a 120MB hard disk, showing that a high-powered machine is advisable, but not always necessary.

Killer Chess II

The Killer Chess II animation was created as part of Mike's A-Level art project on computer graphics. (British A-Levels offer the opportunity for students to earn a type of pre-university degree.) In this reworking of his original Killer Chess animation, Mike took a much more extravagant technical approach. In the original Killer Chess he created the pieces mostly out of distorted spheres, whereas in Killer Chess II he used the Shaper and Lofter much more. For example, Mike used the Fit Deformation tool to create the gold tank and a few other objects. Note that each side has different pieces instead of just differently colored copies. In addition, Mike used individual bitmaps for the paint work on the pieces to give them a high level of detail as Figure 5-13 shows.

Unlike Pinball, Killer Chess II took several months to complete. Consider that the game has 64 moves, each one taking an average of five hours to create (plus time for corrections to parts that failed to come out right the first time). Creating a first pass of Killer Chess II took over 144 hours of time on 3D Studio. When you include the time to create the introduction and finale, as well as build the individual objects, make bitmaps, light the whole scene, and then re-render the moves that didn't come out correctly the first time, you begin to get a feel for the scope of the project.

The opening sequence of the two robots walking to the chess board was created after everything else was done. Not happy with just showing move after move as in the original Killer Chess, Mike wanted to give the sequence a setting. Adding two characters at the beginning of the sequence accomplished this and holds the entire sequence together much

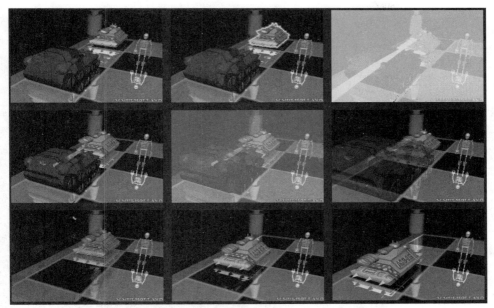

Figure 5-13 A sequence of frames from Killer Chess II

better. Mike's only regret is that he feels that this piece is so large that its size tends to overshadow the technical advances. There are simply so many incredible parts that the complete effect is overwelming.

Killer Chess II was created on a 486/33 with 16MB of memory. The machine was barely able to handle the size of the model, as some renders started to swap out parts of memory to the hard disk. The final 3D Studio project file is over 5MB in size.

Hellfire

Mike's final animation on the CD is the incredible Hellfire. Unlike Killer Chess II, this sequence takes place in a real environment and on a large scale, leaving scope for more complex scenery. As with many of Mike's pieces, this animation saw some drastic changes halfway through. After returning to the nearly completed animation after a five-week break, Mike added more detail to the cockpit area of the helicopter and reworked the blades to rotate more smoothly. One of the most interesting effects results from the beams of light created by applying a glass texture with additive transparency to a simple cone, as shown in Figure 5-14. These cones are then linked to the helicopter so that they highlight the ground and buildings as the sequence progresses, greatly adding to the sense of motion, space, and realism.

Mike created all of the bitmaps using Animator Pro, which he ran from inside 3D Studio to allow instant examination of the results. The floor bitmap is probably the

Figure 5-14 In this shot from Hellfire, note how effectively glass cones with additive transparency create a spotlight effect

most interesting. After creating the city, Mike saved a picture at the highest allowable VESA resolution from the Top view. Since rendering the orthogonal views in 3D Studio delivers an image with no perspective, this file was then loaded into Animator Pro, where roads, pavements, and bushes were added. A bump map was also created based on the Top view to reinforce the feeling of depth.

Tips

Mike thinks his best and oldest trick is to first render a scene without the parts that move, and then use that image as a background. With this technique, you can create incredibly complicated animations on low-powered machines in a fraction of the time they would otherwise take. Carrying this idea one step further, multiple project files are useful, as they allow you to create extremely complex objects while still keeping the memory usage at a reasonable level.

A less obvious trick is to physically mark on the monitor the exact placement of objects. Mike uses water-based magic markers a great deal, particularly if trying to make a character walk without its feet sliding.

If you are doing multiple shots of complex objects you will nearly always have trouble with the palette. This manifests itself by showing a horrible flash as the colors change when you switch between flics. To get around this without sacrificing the quality of the image (as invariably happens when you use a fixed palette), try mixing the palettes using Animator Pro's Blend feature, which you will find under the Palette menu on the Palette Panel. This tool takes a palette in the clipboard and lets you merge it with varying strengths into the palette assigned to the current frame. To merge two flics with radically different palettes, the first step is to join your two flics together. Cut the entire palette from the last frame of the outgoing flic and then blend it with 90 percent strength to the first frame of the incoming flic. Over the next several frames apply Blend in diminishing strength so as to create a change in palette that will be hardly noticeable. The number of frames over which you gradually diminish the strength of the blending will affect the degree of screen flicker caused by changing all of the palette indices simultaneously.

Grahame Naylor

Magic Lantern
London, UK
\NAYLOR*.FLI   19.8MB

Figure 5-15 In TAKEOFF.FLI, the background image has few colors, allowing 3D Studio to apply more of the palette to the plane

Most of Grahame's animation is done for broadcast-quality video. While this is very laborious, it's also quite rewarding because the image quality is so good. However, he still finds a unique excitement in seeing real-time animation on the computer screen.

Both of the animations from Magic Lantern on the CD were originally made as tests before final rendering to video. For the purpose of this publication, they were re-created with CD-based playback in mind. Color ranges were carefully tuned so that the objects of interest would have plenty of shading colors available. For example, you will notice that there are very few grays available for the background walls of OFFICE.FLI. In contrast, the desk and floor shade and animate very well because there were enough shades of brown.

TAKEOFF.FLI

Takeoff, shown in Figure 5-15, is a flic for a new airport development. The 747-400 model is from Viewpoint Animation Engineering. To avoid copyright problems the livery is incomplete, but this isn't a big concern because the airline doesn't fly this model yet anyway. Grahame notes that the whole effect of this animation is greatly enhanced with sound effects. He leaves it as an exercise for the readers to use the multimedia program of their choice to

Figure 5-16 In OFFICE.FLI, motion blur works very well

add a suitable track. The first attempt at making TAKEOFF.FLI didn't work because the sky used the same images for the background as the video version did. While dramatic as a video, it looked terrible on the flic because it needed too many colors. The new sky map works much better because it has less contrast and creates less change from frame to frame. As a result, the animation plays much more smoothly.

OFFICE.FLI

The office scene in Figure 5-16 had been lurking around Grahame's hard disk for some time before he dug it out again as a test piece for 3D Studio Release 3. The objects are from a variety of sources. The basic computer comes from the 3D Studio World-Creating Toolkit CD, but Grahame changed the keyboard so it wouldn't look dated. The desk was from an AutoCAD mesh file supplied by Mathews Office Furniture (as a kind of credit, the book on the desk is their brochure). The chair started life many years ago on TOPAS. Grahame created the excellent CD and CD-ROM drive himself. Check out the great use of motion blur in this animation.

The moral of this flic is that, for architectural animation, it pays to be a bit of a packrat. You never get enough time to make all of the accessories you need.

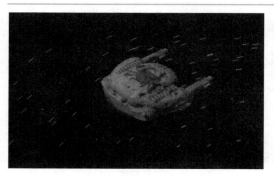

Thomas Reimann

Grueningen, Switzerland
\REIMANN\CRAB7.FLI   13.2MB

Figure 5-17 The CRAB7 space fighter toward the end of the flic

Thomas created the Crab7 animation in Figure 5-17 especially for *Modeling the Dream CD.* Originally, the model was to be used to create an opening for a game, but unfortunately the game's programmer gave up on the project; Thomas is now stuck with great graphics but no programmer to work with.

Thomas feels that the most important thing you need to create exciting 3D animations is a good imagination. To cultivate this, he reads books, watches movies, and generally daydreams a great deal. When he sits down with 3D Studio, he is very careful not to try to create everything in his mind's eye, focusing his priorities to work within the realm of the possible. For him, the first step of creating something like Crab7 is modeling his raw idea and then not being afraid to change it.

Since Thomas is still in school, the creation of pictures and animations such as Crab7 is just a hobby, although he hopes to land a job where he can produce animations like this for a living. For an example of his unusual talents, take a look at the explosion from the final frames of Crab7, shown in Figure 5-18. His technique produces a stunning finale to an amazing sequence.

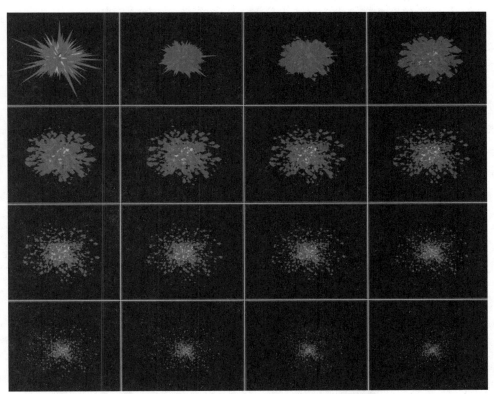

Figure 5-18 The final frames of the explosion of the space fighter

Jeff Rouyer

Longmont, CO, USA
\ROUYER*.FLI   17.7MB

Figure 5-19 This Whirligig animation won the Waite Group's Making Movies contest

This animator has the distinction of winning the Waite Group's Making Movies contest with his phenomenal WHIRLI.FLI. As a wildlife biologist, Jeff spends a great deal of time outdoors working for various agencies of the federal government. Creating animations such as this is a hobby which he claims verges on addiction. Here is a list of the tools that were used:

 POLYRAY v1.7—to generate the ray-traced animation sequences

 DTA v2.1b—to compile all the targa file sequences into a flic

 DMORF v1.12—to morph animation sequences

 AAPLAYHI v1.1—to view flics

 BLOB SCULPTOR v1.0—to build wire frame organic blob shapes for export to ray-tracers

 POVCAD—v 3.0 CAD wire frame program used to build complex Polyray Images

 DYEWORKS v 1.31—for batch color reduction and file conversion

 GRAPHIC WORKSHOP v1.1—also used for color reduction and file conversion

As with traditional hand-drawn animation, Jeff's technique starts with a storyboard (see Figure 5-20). A typical storyboard scene will include a cartoon sketch of the main objects with arrows and notes describing how those objects will move and interact. Each scene key illustrated in the storyboard is then transformed into a file consisting of Polyray code, the separate objects being used created one at a time. Texture, color, and movement attributes are then applied to each object.

Since Polyray uses a programming syntax for defining shapes, colors, and movements, creating complex animations can quickly get complicated. In WHIRLI.FLI, complication is kept to a minimum by copying and then making minor modifications to individual

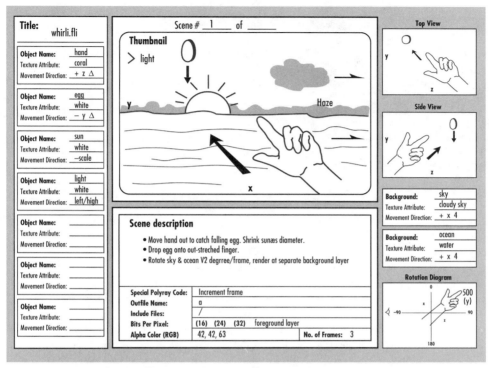

Figure 5-20 Jeff has developed a storyboard format which assists with the placing of objects in Polyray 3D space

scene files. For example, scene < a > in WHIRLI.FLI moves the hand out away from the camera, drops the egg, and rotates the clouds and ocean, all in five sequential frames. Once completed, the scene file < a > is copied to a new file named scene < b >. In scene < b >, the object movement code is modified so that the hand motion is reversed toward the camera and the egg follows the same motion. Once scene < b > is completed, the file is copied to scene < c > and so on. At each successive stage of the process, Jeff limits himself to editing the object movement code, adding new objects, and deleting old objects. WHIRLI.FLI is a composite of 26 key scene files created by the process of progressively copying and modifying scene files. By putting all the rendered scene files together, you get an animation that is continuous and fluid.

Jeff notes that it is possible to make the same animation using a single Polyray file with advanced programming code to move the objects to multiple positions; working through the animation scene by scene is easier to manage for beginners. As your skill with Polyray code develops, you can reduce the number of scene files.

Paul Russam

The Electric Drawing Board
London, UK
\RUSSAM\CHERNOB?.FLI   29.14MB

Figure 5-21 A frame showing the Chernobyl reactor being encased by robots

I have never seen a more significant use of computer multimedia than the Ukritiye Encasement proposal put together by Paul Russam and Ken Kenner of The Electric Drawing Board. In 1992, the Ukrainian government hosted an international competition welcoming plans for how best to convert the current sarcophagus surrounding Chernobyl reactor number four into an ecologically safe system. As part of an international team composed of representatives from Lawrence Livermore National Labs, Carnegie Mellon University, and the office of Prime Minister John Major, Paul and Ken were given the task of creating an animated 3D model to demonstrate a proposal. At the time, they were just starting their business and had been using 3D Studio for only two weeks.

As you can see from the flic, an image from which appears in Figure 5-21, the general idea is to build a latticework of several triangles upon which thick steel plates can be hung. Given the stability with which heavy objects can be hauled from only three control points, this plan is an elegantly simple solution to the problem of encasement with minimal danger to the workforce.

This file was originally a 180MB Animator Pro script file, which was converted down to 320x200 resolution using Animator Pro's Shrink 2x feature. All of the component files were then concatenated together, leaving an acceptable representation of their original proposal that certainly plays back at a more acceptable speed from CD-ROM.

The final sequence of this animation shows the reactor lid (weighing over 2000 tons) being extracted from what is left of the reactor core. When Chernobyl exploded, this lid was blown up into the air like a champagne cork, rotating 270 degrees in the air before landing back inside the reactor vessel. Because this lid is so precariously balanced at present, its removal is essential once the reactor is completely enclosed.

Paul offers the following tip to those trying to assemble something from a number of parts in 3D Studio: Rather than trying to get pieces to fly into place, start with the finished object and then dismantle it. Using Animator Pro, it's quite easy to just save the rendered animation backwards, creating a smooth assembly.

Animations Created with Ray Tracing Programs

3D Studio isn't the only game in town when it comes to producing 3D animations on the PC. For those with an inclination toward mathematics, a number of excellent shareware tools produce amazing results. Two of the finest are POV-Ray and Polyray. This section showcases some of the finer examples of work produced with these tools and fills you in on the artists responsible.

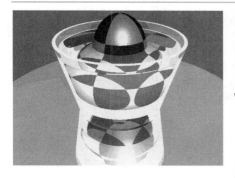

David Bleecker

Department of Mathematics
University of Hawaii
Honolulu, HI USA
\MAKEMOVE\GLASSP30.FLC   0.9MB

Figure 5-22 GLASSP30.FLC—Waiter, There's a Zonal Harmonic in my Glass

A number of flics on the CD were sent into Waite Group Press by readers of David Mason's and Alexander Enzmann's *Making Movies on Your PC*. This book and disk combination contains all the tools necessary to create amazing 3D animations, and a prize was offered for the best flics received. A screenshot from David Bleecker's entry is shown in Figure 5-22.

In GLASSP30, P30 stands for the third zonal spherical harmonic. This harmonic determines a vibrational mode in which the northern and southern hemispheres of a sphere alternately become larger and smaller. In the movie, the sphere has been placed in a glass of liquid, and the water level lowers when the top hemisphere expands and the lower hemisphere shrinks. The glass sits on a round mirrored table, which demonstrates the ability of Polyray to handle reflections. The liquid and the glass show Polyray's multiple refraction capabilities.

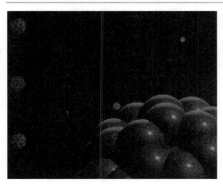

Dan Richardson

Northhampton, MA, USA
\RICHARDS\BUCKA640.FLC   12.20MB

Figure 5-23 The Buckminsterfullerene molecule as modeled in BUCKA640.FLC

Dan is a digital illustrator specializing in the production of images for medical and scientific publishers. He is also the author of *Create Stereograms on Your PC* (Waite Group Press, 1994). He works primarily in POV-Ray and RenderMan, with data from various chemical modelers and university databases. Producing animations such as BUCKA640.FLC (Figure 5-23) is a hobby to, as he puts it, use up excess CPU cycles and data storage space.

This 1,080-frame flic represents the structure of a C60 molecule that goes by the name of Buckminsterfullerene, or "buckyball" for short. The buckyball was built in DesignCAD 3D and then rendered in a beta version of POV-Ray 2.0 using a custom iridescence texture developed by Merlin Farmer. As far as POV-Ray is concerned, the buckyball is declared as an object in the scene file with a red light in the center. This declared object is then instanced 26 times with various transformations and rotations. POV's *clock* variable is used as a multiplier in many of the transformations and rotations, as shown in Listing 5-1. Being a fan of compact code, Dan is proud to point out that the entire POV-Ray data file for buckyball is only 8K and 196 lines long, with no include files needed—and 65 lines of that is the declaration of the buckyball object.

Listing 5-1 Using POV's clock variable

```
object { buckyball    //big one which enters the foreground
rotate < clock*3/2, 0, 0 >
translate < 0, 60, 0 >
rotate < 0, 0, (clock/4) -50 >
rotate > 0, 85, 0 >}
```

Each of the 26 buckyballs contains a light, so each becomes a multiple-beam searchlight as it tumbles and orbits. There is also a weak ambient light, but most of the scene is illuminated by these flashing, moving, searchlight beams.

The animation was rendered from a batch file which calls POV 1,080 times, incrementing the clock variable by a third of a degree and providing a new sequential output filename each call, as shown in Listing 5-2. The title screen was created with Picture Publisher 4, which has a lovely anti-aliased text feature. The final .FLC file was assembled and matted in David Mason's DTA 2.05. The 267x200 image size was chosen to produce a 12 to 14 MB flic, which is as large an animation as could be played from RAM on Dan's 16MB machine. The animation was then matted into the 640x480 title frame using DTA.

Listing 5-2 Part of the batch file that runs Buckyball

```
povray -ibucka640.pov -oanim0010.tga +k001.0
povray -ibucka640.pov -oanim0013.tga +k001.33
povray -ibucka640.pov -oanim0016.tga +k001.66
povray -ibucka640.pov -oanim0020.tga +k002.0
povray -ibucka640.pov -oanim0023.tga +k002.33
povray -ibucka640.pov -oanim0026.tga +k002.66
povray -ibucka640.pov -oanim0030.tga +k003.0
```

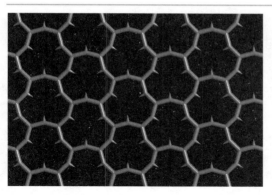

Chris Young

Indianapolis, IN, USA
\YOUNG*.FLI   7.64MB

Figure 5-24 The Hexpanding Universe

Chris Young is a coauthor of the Waite Group Press' bestselling book *Ray Tracing Creations*. The Hexpanding Universe is a 640x480 flic consisting of 60 frames (one of which is shown in Figure 5-24) that shows a slowly rotating grid of hexagons set in front of a star-filled sky. The grid grows, subdivides, and grows again in an infinite pattern of expansion and fractal growth.

The original idea came from a simple illustration of fractal subdivision in the book *Computer Graphics Principals and Practices, 2nd Edition* by Foley, Van Dam, Feiner, and Hughes. It noted that a hexagon can be subdivided into three similar hexagons by adding three new lines and bending all six sides.

The hexagon slowly grows until it gets too large. The sides of the hexagons then bend in the center, with three sides bending inwards and three bending outwards. At each breaking point, a bud is sprouted and begins to grow. Three buds eventually touch and grow together. The deformed hexagon with the three full-grown buds transforms itself into three new, small hexagons that continue to grow and subdivide in an infinite loop. The entire grid also rotates to add to the dynamic nature of this network of ever-expanding hexagons.

The complex rotations of individual elements was difficult to implement because Chris wasn't exactly sure what motions were necessary. He knew what the beginning of a sequence should look like, as well as the end. Based upon these, he created test renderings. After a five or ten frame test, he'd discover that the path from A to B wasn't correct when the pieces seemed to fly apart and then magically fall into place.

In the end, a hierarchy of rotations and translations was used to keep all of the joints connected. Chris began by animating a single rod inside the hexagon as it bends and sprouts a bud. However, three sides had to bend in and three had to bend out. Initially, he simply rotated the rod 180 degrees, but the recursive application of this had unwanted side effects later. To solve this problem, he had to create a Rod A that bent one way and a Rod B that bent the other. The rods were connected together in sequence so that successive pieces would bend but stay together. It's like bending your shoulder, elbow, wrist and fingers by different amounts simultaneously. The resulting motion of your fingertip would be hard to describe.

Chris Young in His Own Words

I am self-employed as a programmer, consultant, and technical writer. I am the team coordinator for the POV-Ray team. This all-volunteer group has developed one of the most powerful PC-based rendering programs available anywhere: The Persistence of Vision Ray Tracer. We distribute it as copyrighted freeware. It is written in highly portable C and has been compiled on everything from Atari to Cray computers. We distribute executable versions for IBM, Mac, and Amiga. I designed and implemented the improvements and specifications to the POV-Ray language version 2.0.

I have a form of muscular dystrophy and have never walked. While growing up, I had limited use of my hands, but I enjoyed creating things with my hands, such as balsa-wood model airplanes and rockets. I didn't have sufficient strength to work modeling clay, so sculpting was beyond me. Therefore, I was always fascinated by ways to represent 3D objects in accurate 2D images. I tried sketching, but I couldn't figure out why my drawings looked distorted. Artists paint or draw on an easel, so that their view is perpendicular to the page. I could only draw with the paper lying flat. When viewed from exactly eye-level, my sketches had reasonably good perspective, but when viewed straight on, they looked awful. I gave up. Later my strength deteriorated further and now I can no longer draw at all.

My chosen vocation of programmer, consultant, and author is not beyond my physical limitations because I use a personal computer. I type by standing the keyboard up on an easel and poking at the keys with what is left of the strength in my right hand. Eventually I'll lose that ability, too. However, alternative devices are available for people with handicaps more severe than mine. The computer allows me to do productive work despite my physical limitations. Via modem I am able to collaborate with POV-Ray team members coast-to-coast and as far away as Germany and Australia without leaving my office in my home in Indianapolis.

I've never met face-to-face with my coauthor or publisher in California. Using tools like POV-Ray and my PC, I am similarly freed from my physical limitations in my pursuit of artistic expression. Computer art has the potential to tap the artistic souls of people who would otherwise have no outlet for their creative energies. We know from examples like Nobel laureate Stephen J. Hawkings that genius can reside in a severely handicapped body. Perhaps computer art will someday uncover the stifled artistic genius of a physically handicapped Picasso or Michelangelo. If my contributions as a developer of computer graphic software and my meager artistic tinkering can pave the way for such talent to shine forth, I will be very proud. Until then, I'm having fun ray tracing and helping others to have fun, too.

CHAPTER 6
Sound
Blaster Demos

Y ou've reached the part of the book where the really flashy stuff is kept. This chapter covers demonstration material designed to be run with audio cards such as the Creative Labs Sound Blaster and the Gravis UltraSound. The main features of this chapter are the rocking, custom-coded, assembly language demos coming out of Northern Europe. You'll be introduced to the leading teams and get some hints on how they tweak the lowest level of the machine to produce incredible effects. In addition, you'll find a collection of sound bites from Niko Boese, as well as a fully working but limited version of Kaleidosonics from Masque Publishing.

If you jumped directly to this chapter, you missed the two BigDemos which are the largest programs on the CD to drive your audio card. To read about these 30-minute, 140MB demos, turn back to Chapter 3.

 ## The Demo Scene

A cult following known as The Scene has taken off in Northern Europe. In its loosest form, The Scene is held together by hundreds of BBS systems connected through the Creativity Demo Net. Messages and binary files move among people on the network practically for free as each BBS automatically calls others to exchange mail. While this practice has been around for years in an incarnation known as FidoNet, a group of BBS sysops active in The Scene started up their own network in August 1992 to keep their mail from getting lost in other traffic.

The Scene gets serious for their international gatherings held three to four times a year. These gatherings are opportunities for programmers and artists to meet and share ideas, but the primary events are the competitions. There are different categories for music, graphics, and intros (demos smaller than 100K) as well as a main demo contest. There are separate categories for the PC, Atari ST, and Amiga, with each event having up to 15 entrants, so judging can take a couple of days. Anyone who pays the admission fee can cast a vote in any of the categories. The prizes consist of cash (generated by admission fees) and products (donated by sponsors).

In the case of the PC, all entries are played back from a standard 486 attached to a large projector and a powerful sound system. Contestants are free to boot DOS in any configuration they choose. While this complete lack of any standardization gives developers the freedom to drive the machine in any way they please, it can create horrendous runtime problems. For example, some demos require excessively large amounts of conventional memory, while others need a memory manager such as QEMM to be loaded. For this reason, most demos are never released at the competitions where they are first shown; the developers usually need another month or two to iron out the bugs and allow their demos to run under a wider range of circumstances.

There is a bit of hero-worship at these events. Attendees revere the programmers who work out exciting new effects. Combining the work of graphic artists, animators and musicians using nothing more than an assembler earns these individuals a great deal of respect. But the programmers don't work alone; these productions are very much team efforts. In the pages that follow, when the name of an individual is presented, keep in mind that this person probably represents a group, and therefore is not necessarily the programming genius responsible for producing the entire presentation.

To appreciate the work of the artists in this chapter, you need to understand that the computer for the most part generates the graphics in real time. Precalculated animations such as those presented in Chapter 5 are a whole other animal. While almost any experienced PC user can, in time, begin producing animations using 3D Studio, very few people can master the "black art" of custom-coding the VGA and supporting sound hardware to squeeze the maximum performance from the machine. So, when you run the Elements demo by Xography, for example, keep in mind that it would take 3D Studio a few days to generate a flic file that contained all the frames this program is building on the fly.

To round out the collection we conclude with a working version of some neat relaxation-therapy software, as well as a collection of audio clips for your listening pleasure.

Running the Hottest Demos

The CD includes over a dozen of the best demos The Scene has to offer. Each of them has been thoroughly tested for reliability and should run with no problems if you follow the instructions and use the boot disk when needed. Since many of these programs utilize large amounts of memory and are particularly picky about the configuration of your machine, viewing them without a boot disk can be rather tedious. To simplify things, the menu system

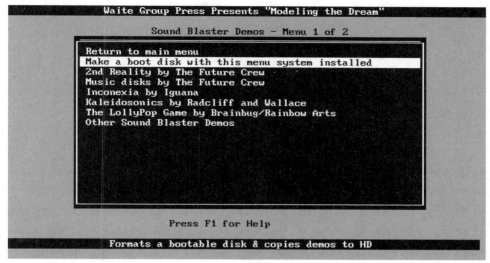

Figure 6-1 The Sound Blaster Demos menu with the boot disk generation option chosen

provides the capability to reboot your computer from floppy in such a way that the menu system still comes up. Instead of accessing the demos from CD, when you use the boot floppy, they are loaded from your hard disk. This procedure can be accessed by choosing the boot disk generation option, as Figure 6-1 shows.

The boot disk is necessary because almost everyone runs their computer with some type of memory management software. Programs such as EMM386, QEMM, or 386 to the Max have the effect of changing the mode in which your processor is running. Many of the demos in this section require that your processor be in native "protected mode," allowing memory beyond DOS's normal 640K to be readily available. By putting a PC in virtual 8088 mode, memory managers restrict these programs' ability to directly access this memory. Rather than have their demos run slowly, developers included here have chosen to prevent their demos from running at all in virtual modes, making the boot disk necessary.

The Boot Disk Generation Procedure

The boot disk procedure carries out the following steps, in order:

1. Asks you to select a drive to temporarily hold the demo programs. No more than 12MB of data will be copied to your hard disk.

2. Formats a bootable floppy disk with the necessary DOS files.

3. Builds the menu system on the floppy so that the demos on the hard disk can be easily accessed.

4. Copies the demos to hard disk.

After you have rebooted your computer from the floppy, the menu system will load, allowing you access to these programs. The final menu option on the boot floppy menu deletes the demos from your hard disk for you.

Some of these demos take over your system on a very low level and require you to press the reset button to end the demo. When this is the case it has been noted under the demo's heading. In other cases simply press (ESC) to quit.

Our Favorites

Table 6-1 lists what we believe are the top four demos in this chapter. As you can see three of these require that no memory manager be installed. The fourth, Second Reality, will run just fine as long as your system has more than 570K of free conventional memory as well as 2MB of EMS. To get started with the Sound Blaster demos, select *Demos for the Sound Blaster* from the main menu.

Title of Demo	Name of Group	File name on CD	Memory Configuration
Second Reality	Future Crew	2NDREAL.EXE	570K conventional, 2MB EMS
Elements	Xography	ELEMENTS.EXE	Needs protected mode
Inconexia	Iguana	INCONEXI.EXE	Prefers protected mode
Hex Appeal	Cascada	APPEAL.EXE	Prefers protected mode

Table 6-1 Memory needs of selected demos

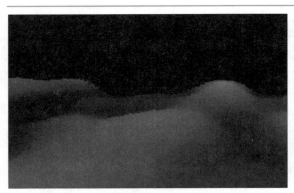

Samuli Syvahuoko–
The Future Crew

Espoo, Finland
2NDREAL.EXE
JOURNEY1.EXE
JOURNEY2.EXE
CHMIND.EXE
MENTAL_S.ARJ
SCRNT301.EXE

Figure 6-2 The morphing 3D landscape from Second Reality

Members of The Future Crew are the undisputed kings of the demo world. This group of nine young people ranging in age from 17 to 21 has consistently won the majority of prizes at most demo competitions for being able to pull off incredible effects such as the morphing 3D landscape in Figure 6-2. You can learn pretty much everything you want to know about them in the file FCINFO13.TXT that you will find in the file 2NDREAL.EXE on the disc.

For beginning programmers interested in learning how to code demos, The Future Crew recommends the following:

 Become familiar with a high-level language such as C or Pascal before experimenting with assembler. The Future Crew uses Borland Turbo Assembler as well as Borland C++.

 Examine the file MENTAL_S.ARJ in the \SBDEMOS directory that contains the Mental Surgery demo. This early demo by The Future Crew was released with full source code for the STMIK (Scream Tracker Music Interface Kit). You can link this four-channel music player for the Sound Blaster into your own programs. (The documentation of this source code is extremely sparse, so proceed at your own risk.) Also, check out the contents of SCRMT301.EXE, which contains the Scream Tracker 3 music engine.

 Appendix C provides a list of books that The Future Crew uses as reference materials. They advise, however, that reading is no substitute for trying out new ideas. There is no magic way of learning how to code; it takes hard work and years of practice.

Second Reality—2NDREAL.EXE

The Future Crew's latest demo as of this writing is Second Reality, shots of which can be seen in Figure 6-3 and Figure 6-4. To see this piece at its best, you should have a 486-based machine and a sound card. The Future Crew prefers the Gravis UltraSound because it uses much less CPU time than the Sound Blaster. Second Reality requires 570K bytes of free conventional memory. If you are using a Sound Blaster or Sound Blaster Pro, you will need an additional 1MB of expanded memory.

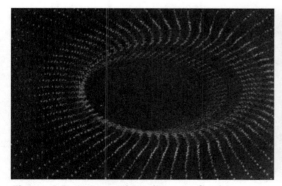

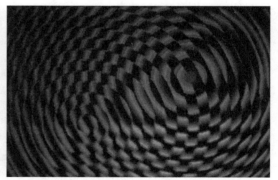

Figure 6-3 In Second Reality you fly down this tunnel to a rocking sound track

Figure 6-4 These flying concentric circles morph and reform at incredibly high rates of speed

Select your sound card and the mixing frequency you want from the Setup screen. If you have a Dolby Surround decoder and amplifier handy, this demo will create some fantastic 3D sound effects for your listening pleasure by entering subtle delays into the sound to create a surrounding effect. For some reason, these effects are not very clear when playing out of the Sound Blaster Pro or Sound Blaster 16 but amazing on the Gravis UltraSound.

You can pass Second Reality numbers on the command line in order to have it start from different places; for example, type

👉 **SECOND /2** (ENTER) to start the demo from the title screen. Similarly,

👉 **SECOND /3** will start from the landscape scroller.

👉 **SECOND /4** will start from the vector graphics.

👉 **SECOND /5** will start from the end credits.

If you want to run this demo in an endless loop, just enable the looping option at the Setup screen. In this mode, the demo will start again without rolling the long sequence of credits at the end.

The Music Disk Program—CHMIND.EXE, JOURNEY?.EXE

CHMIND.EXE, JOURNEY1.EXE, and JOURNEY2.EXE contain songs created with the Music Disk Player program released as freeware by The Future Crew. The MDP program is not meant to have any flashy graphics. Instead, it performs the functions of a jukebox with a graphic equalizer. It supports only two music file formats: the popular MOD, which originated on the Amiga, and the Scream Tracker (S3M) a music format developed by The Future Crew. Upon executing MDP.EXE, the program will auto-detect a Sound Blaster or Gravis UltraSound card. If for some reason the program has trouble finding your audio card, type **MDP** (ENTER) for information on overriding the auto-detection. You will also find a control for varying the mixing speed at which the music is generated. Warning: Play with this feature at your own risk. Entering the wrong values can crash the system.

One of the nice features of MDP is that, if you get tired of looking at the on-screen music tracker shown in Figure 6-5, you can press (F7) to return to DOS. Playing music with MDP in resident mode on the Sound Blaster appears to consume only a very small amount of CPU resources. The Norton utility SYSINFO rated a 486/66 PC running the MDP program in resident mode as having 75 times the performance of an IBM PC, as opposed to the normal reading of 100 times. To add your own MOD or S3M files to the playlist, just edit the file MDP.MDI. If you want more information on this program, the file MDP.DOC located in the JOURNEY?.EXE archives is quite thorough.

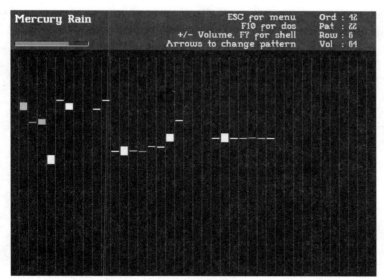

Figure 6-5 The "tracker" screen from the
Music Disk Program

Timo Ludwig—Xography

Dielheim, Germany
ELEMENTS.EXE
Boot disk recommended
Press reset button to quit

Figure 6-6 Elements features texture
mapped graphics calculated on the fly

Xography (pronounced *sog-raf-ee*) makes its debut on The Scene with the Elements demo, with its incredible real-time texture mapped graphics. The lead programmer, Thomas Walther, has achieved a real breakthrough with this piece. As with so much of this material, there is an abundance of reflective spheres and throbbing techno music, but what makes Elements so unique is the number of materials that are mapped to surfaces on the fly. The flythrough of the cityscape shown in Figure 6-6 is particularly remarkable.

To run Elements, you need 486/33 or better with at least 610K of free conventional memory and 1MB of free XMS. If configuring your PC with this much free RAM is a hassle, just generate the boot disk for viewing protected-mode demos and give your machine the "three fingered salute." Don't even think of running this on a 486SX class machine; it runs too slowly, particularly if you are using a Sound Blaster. The creators strongly recommend that you use a Gravis UltraSound (GUS).

Like many other demos, Elements will attempt to detect your sound card. In some cases, this auto-detection is going to fail, particularly if you have a number of other cards in your machine. If you have any trouble getting this demo to work with your sound card, try setting an MPDEVICE environment variable to override auto-detection. You will have to do this at the DOS command line, but it isn't that difficult if you type carefully. The syntax for setting the MPDEVICE environment variable is as follows:

```
MPDEVICE=<card>,<base address>,<IRQ>, <DMA>, <RAMSIZE || MIXRATE>
```

where

- Card 0 = Gravis Ultra Sound, 1 = Sound Blaster, 2 = Sound Blaster Pro
- Base Address = The value of the port in hex
- IRQ = Hardware interrupt used
- DMA = DMA channel used
- RAMSIZE = If card is GUS, the amount of memory onboard on the GUS
- MIXRATE = If card is a Sound Blaster, the amount of CPU resources to spend mixing the music

Consider these two sample lines:

```
SET MPDEVICE=1,220,7,1,22050
SET MPDEVICE=0,220,7,7,512
```

The first example tells Elements to expect a Sound Blaster on port 220h, IRQ7, DMA 1, and to run with a mixing rate of 22Khz. The second one tells Elements to use a Gravis UltraSound with 512K of RAM on port 220h, IRQ7, DMA 7.

Erik Stridell—Cascada

Surahammar, Sweden
APPEAL.EXE

Figure 6-7 In the HexAppeal setup screen, you don't have to worry about setting an I/O address

The members of Cascada thought it was time to take a break from all of the recent "techno" soundtracks and have come up with something much more mellow. The soothing graphics and sounds aren't quite as laid-back as Amnesia from Renaissance on the first *Walkthroughs & Flybys CD,* but are definitely a step in that direction.

Appeal will run on machines with XMS memory, so loading HIMEM.SYS in your CONFIG.SYS file is fine. However, if you use a memory manager such as QEMM or EMM386, use the boot disk generation option.

Figure 6-7 shows the Appeal setup screen. If you use a Sound Blaster, you don't need to specify an I/O address. If you are using a Gravis UltraSound, be sure that it is properly initialized with ULTRINIT.EXE. The developers are particularly proud of the quality of their player for the UltraSound, hence its position at the top of the list of recommended sound devices. If you have a fast machine, be sure to turn on the sampling interpolation feature to radically improve the sound quality. The demo will probably run slower as a result however, particularly if you have a Sound Blaster instead of a GUS. If this demo doesn't run smoothly for you, turning this option off is the first thing you should try.

All the effects you see are calculated in real time by your processor. The underlying code is pure assembly language compiled under Borland Turbo Assembler. The effects were made by several programmers who each made small routines while taking a break from other projects. In the summer of 1993, these effects were consolidated into a demo with the addition of new graphics and a soundtrack. Cascada relies on Borland products for the programming, Deluxe Paint from Electronic Arts for the graphics, and the Triton Fastracker and Audio View by Voyetra for the sound.

Iguana/VangeliSTeam

Juan Carlos Arevalo
Inconexia
Madrid, Spain
INCONEXI.EXE
Boot disk recommended
Press (ESC) to advance

Figure 6-8 The opening logo for Inconexia gently fades out against a background of stars

There is an exotic feel to Inconexia; perhaps the graphics and music have been softened by a Latin touch. The demo opens with a 3D logo that gently bursts onto the screen and then fades away into the background starfield, which you can see in Figure 6-8.

When it comes to real-time texture mapped graphics, this crew takes an interesting twist by using pictures from the grand masters to adorn the walls (see Figure 6-9).

The third image of this demo, shown in Figure 6-10, shows off the speed at which 12 or so spheres zip around the screen. When they collide, the spheres bounce off one another with great realism. This image was shot on 400 ASA film with the shutter open for 0.15 seconds.

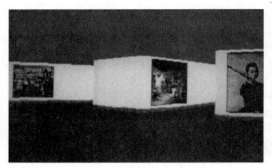

Figure 6-9 You'll fly down these museum corridors faster than you believed was possible

Figure 6-10 Over a dozen spheres bounce around the screen during one part of Inconexia

Figure 6-11 The Debut logo from DarkZone

Thomas Hellesen– DarkZone

Rykkinn, Norway
DZDEBUT.EXE
GOURFACE.EXE
Boot disk recommended for Debut
Press reset button to quit Debut

Debut

Debut (Figure 6-11) is a great little demo, or *intro,* as the small ones are called. It only supports the Gravis UltraSound, so if you have another audio card, just choose option five at the I/O address prompt. Debut requires a 386 CPU or higher with a standard VGA card. It makes no use of a math coprocessor so the speed of the animation is entirely dependent on the clock speed and video implementation of your PC. This makes it an excellent demo to run on new hardware to gauge system performance. It runs fine from inside of Windows in Full Screen mode with the Exclusive Foreground option selected.

This demo has wicked effects. In the "dot vector morph" 3,600 dots whirl through 3D space, swimming and reforming into various objects. The screen resolution is set at 320x400, which is one of the undocumented video modes favored by graphics hacks everywhere. The main appeal of this graphics mode is that it offers twice the vertical resolution of standard 320x200 mode and still allows multiple pages of memory to be flipped through very quickly.

Thomas used standard assembler routines for the rotation, but the optimization lies in using 32-bit assembler code that makes use of all the segment registers (DS ES FS GS) as well as all the general-purpose registers (SI DI AX BX CX DX BP SP). His trick in creating the fast and smooth 9,096-dot pixel tunnel is to precalculate six frames, each with a different rotation step, and then snap rapidly between them, only adjusting the center point.

While Thomas created most of the effects and original illustrations, credit also goes to Harold Mathisen for the filled 3D polygon sequence and the psychedelic circles that appear at the end of the demo. Christer Borge Lunde composed the music. If you get a chance to hear this on the GUS, you'll marvel at the close timing of the music to the animations.

Gourface

Gourface (shown in Figure 6-12) is an example of real-time Gouraud rendering written completely in assembler. (The term *Gouraud shading* describes a type of 3D rendering that smooths the edges of adjacent polygons, creating natural-looking contours.) This effect is a preview from a forthcoming demo, so no sound effects accompany the graphics. Like Debut, this demo requires a 386 or better and a standard VGA card.

DarkZone now produce demos purely for the fun and challenge, but they are interested in taking on serious, paying projects. By the time this reaches the shelves, they will doubtless be well on their way to greater challenges.

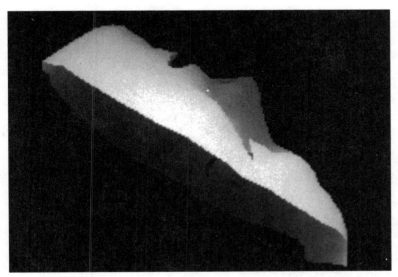

Figure 6-12 Gourface demonstrates real-time Gouraud shading

Figure 6-13 The BrainBug logo comes to life in BRAINBUG.EXE

BrainBug

Ole Mogensen
Aarhus, Denmark
BRAINBUG.EXE
LOLLYPOP.EXE
T3_1.EXE
T3_2.EXE

The four people behind BrainBug are all 23 years old, but have several years in the software development business. Initially, they were hired individually by other companies to write games, but have recently started producing them together as a company. Their snazzy logo, shown in Figure 6-13, really comes to life when you run the BRAINBUG.EXE program. This tiny 18K executable does some morphs that shouldn't be missed. You will also enjoy the two intros from their upcoming game Turrican 3, which at present is a very popular game on the Amiga. But the jewel in their crown right now is Lollypop.

Lollypop

Their largest project at present is a game called "Lollypop." You can see the opening screen of the game in Figure 6-14. Be forewarned that the preview of this game is totally addictive. Set in a toy factory, the star of the game is a little doll called Lolly who comes alive after having been hit by lightning. Your mission as the player is to help her find the candy.

On the technical side, check out the parallax scrolling routines used in this game. When Lolly is moved too near the edge of the screen, the entire display shifts with at least three

Figure 6-14 The opening screen for the Lollypop game preview. It's addictive, so watch out!

transparent levels moving seamlessly. The overall quality of the programming, art, music, and storyline combine to make a first-class game. Unfortunately, you will only get sound from a Sound Blaster if you have it configured for IRQ7. Ole Mogensen at BrainBug points out that this has been fixed for the release version of the game.

Here's what the keys do when you play the game:

 (ALT) starts the game from opening screen

 (→) moves Lolly right

 (←) moves Lolly left

 (↑) makes Lolly jump

Surprise!Productions

Erik Pojar, Vienna, Austria
Ulrik Henriksen, Viby, Denmark
COPPER.EXE
GOODBADU.EXE
Press the reset button to quit Copper

In terms of number of members and international distribution, Suprise!Productions (S!P) is the largest demo group in the world. Over the last four years they have grown from three to over 25 members and are located in Austria, Australia, Denmark, France and Switzerland. They are very proud to have had demos in the top-ten rankings of all the demo "charts" for over a year now. S!P has already produced two games (Whales's Voyage and Super-Nibbly) and is actively seeking commercial projects.

The Austrian section is headed up by Erik Pojar, who works under the alias of "Rick Dangerous." He describes S!P Austria as a bunch of friends who like to program their computers together. They all met at school and are currently studying computer science together in Vienna.

The group does all of their coding in assembly language because the added flexibility gives them total control of the computer. Sometimes they use a BASIC program to precalculate a sine table or other type of dataset, but generally everything is done at the lowest level of the machine.

Copper—Hardware Effects for the Tseng 4000

Copper is unique in that it requires virtually no processing power to create astonishing effects. Although parts of it work only on certain VGAs, such as those based on the very common Tseng 4000 chipset, we have included it for its novelty. If your PC has an acceleration chip built into the video subsystem, then there is a strong chance that parts of this demo will fail to work on your machine.

Figure 6-15 The "Copper effect" is named after a custom graphics chip on the Amiga

The effects you will see in this demo are based on the "Copper effect," a screen shot of which can be seen in Figure 6-15. To understand the significance of the Copper effect, you have to know a bit about how data is displayed on your monitor. A cathode ray starts in the upper-left hand corner of the screen and traverses each scan line, changing color as it goes. When it reaches the lower-right corner, the process repeats itself. Copper does its magic by waiting for the ray to reach a particular scan line before changing the color of the ray. By changing this value at just the right time, it's possible to create high-speed parallel vertical bars using very little CPU time. In fact, this demo will even run on an IBM XT, because most of the time the program is simply waiting for the cathode ray to advance to the next scan line. This demo uses an Adlib player for the sound output. The music and the player were created by Jesper Olsen of the group Vibrants. The graphics were drawn by Peter "J.O.E." Baumstadter.

The Good, the Bad, and the Ugly

The latest demo from Surprise!Productions requires a Gravis UltraSound for output. While this makes the process of coding the demo easier, it certainly limits the audience. By choosing to go with just the UltraSound, however, S!P makes an impressive display of synchronizing the audio with the graphics. This demo makes heavy use of the Copper effect described in the previous section, but there are a number of other spectacular features. Most notable among these are the dot-morphing effects that occur while various 3D objects rotate on the screen. Notice during the dot tunnel toward the end of the demo that not only do the pixels change color as they grow closer, but that they also grow larger. Again, this is a very efficient piece of work and will even run on a 286-based PC.

Sami Kapanen—Epical

Huutomaki, Finland
TAKEOVER.EXE
TANGLE.EXE
Press reset button to quit Takeover

The people behind Epical are young, but have turned out quite a bit of material over the last two years. The six members range in age from 16 to 18, each of them having clearly defined roles. They stress that without teamwork they could never construct the complicated programs and fast effects that go into their demos. When asked why they go to all the trouble, the resounding response is, "Because it's fun!" They take great pride in creating programs that people enjoy. Another major factor is the element of competition among the various groups. Sami believes that there are now hundreds of these demo groups, and their numbers are rapidly growing.

Takeover

TAKEOVER.EXE is the first large, multipart demo by this group. Completed in late 1992, it's one of the oldest demos in this book. While not of the caliber of pieces from The Future Crew or Xography, it is still a fine example of a cooperative effort by a group of very young programmers, artists, and musicians.

While the moving starfields and undulating colored bars appear in many demos, this one's catchy tune and chatty style make it worth watching. Press the (ESC) key at any time to move on to new sections. In the second section, colored blobs move around on the screen (see Figure 6-16) in a common effect known as "shadebobs." The third section has a pulsing onscreen "tracker" to show the levels of the various channels throbbing to the music. After that, you can see an assortment of effects before the credits start to roll.

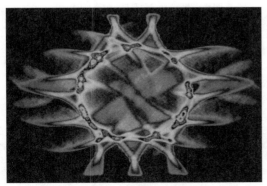

Figure 6-16 The "shadebobs" from Takeover

You can run this demo with a memory manager such as EMM386.EXE installed, despite what the opening message says. On a 486/66 there was no noticeable speed degradation with a memory manager installed.

Niko Boese—Troubadix Studios
Hamburg, Germany
DREAM*.VOC 4.7MB

Niko's contributions to the CD are digitized sound bites that he has created with his Sound Blaster 16. A former employee of one of the largest Creative Labs distributors, at present he offers a composing service mixing clips together for a variety of clients. So far he has produced music for theater performances, video projects, and radio spots.

Table 6-2 lists Niko's sound files which you can find in the \SBDEMOS\BOESE directory. These sampled audio .VOC files have all been recorded with Sound Blaster 16 card at 22kHz mono, so they play back just fine even with the original Sound Blaster. Dream 12 and Dream 13 both utilize a feature of the Creative Labs' .VOC file format that allows you to set blocks to repeat. In other words a subset of a sample can repeat a number of times automatically without the intervention of the program currently running. The VEDIT2.EXE program that ships with the Sound Blaster can be used to set repeat blocks in the .VOC file.

File	Size	Contents
DREAM_01	270052	Jingle with slogan "modeling the dream"
DREAM_02	297052	Same jingle without voice
DREAM_03	182542	Radio jingle
DREAM_04	269905	Sound trailer for TV discussion "Crossfire" (RTL Germany)
DREAM_05	420444	Spot created for Creative Labs' Sound Blaster
DREAM_06	818931	Multimedia advertisement for a fair in Germany
DREAM_07	489844	Spot created for Sound Blaster
DREAM_08	278169	Beginning of the song "Radiation"
DREAM_09	325898	Ending of the song "International"
DREAM_10	132726	"Tell me if there's a way"
DREAM_11	134993	"I still hope"
DREAM_12	54377	Looped part of a song
DREAM_13	62771	Looped part of a song
DREAM_14	284066	"Hey adman"
DREAM_15	361048	Verse 1 of the song "International"
DREAM_16	366058	Verse 3 of the song "International"

Table 6-2 Niko's sound files

If you would like to mix your own jingles and sound bites, Niko recommends getting the following things:

- Sequencer software to manage recorded MIDI data
- MIDI master keyboard to play the desired notes
- Various sound-reproducing devices, such as samplers and synthesizers
- At least one excellent microphone
- Mixing console
- Multi-track tape deck
- Master tape deck, such as a DAT
- Friendly or deaf neighbors

Rob Wallace—The Multimedia Kaleidosonics

Glendale, Arizona, USA
KALEIDOS.EXE

Figure 6-17 The packaging from Kaleidosonics

The Kaleidosonics demo was a collaboration between Rob Wallace, composer extraordinaire, and John Ratcliff, a games and graphics programming guru of the first order. It's actually an example of what is known as *bannerware,* fully working but limited versions of programs released by their authors in a freely distributable form, to increase sales of their product. The actual name of the product is Multimedia Kaleidosonics, published by Masque. (See Appendix C for contact information.) Read the file README.PRN in the KALEIDOS.EXE file for more detail than is presented here.

Kaleidosonics is interactive art and relaxation software. You witness hundreds of visual effects, such as the one shown in Figure 6-17, against six different backgrounds moving to an original soundtrack. The graphics onscreen use a variety of techniques, such as texture mapping, image warping, and fractal image recursion to grab and hold your attention. The overall effect is such that one user comments, "After running Kaleidosonics for just an hour I felt so relaxed that I wanted to take the whole day off."

When you run Kaleidosonics from the menu system, the files will unpack to your hard disk, and a file called SETUP.EXE will configure the program to run with your sound card. This program might look familiar to you because it is the precursor to the driver set up used for The BigDemo. For more information on the underlying device-independent sound card drivers, be sure to read about DIGPAK and MIDPAK in Chapter 3.

Be sure that your (NUM LOCK) key is turned off before you start Kaleidosonics. Table 6-3 shows how keys noted in Table 6-3 affect the operation of the program.

Key	Result
A/a	Toggle auto-advance mode
B/b	Advance to next/return to previous bitmap for 3D models
C/c	Toggle MIDI music on and off
D/d	Toggle dim mode on/off; controls whether or not lead sphere or circle is dimmed
E/e	Anchor the current image in the middle of the screen
F/f	"Fix it." This key resets the current picture, turning all effects off
G/g	Cancel zooming effect/Increase zooming speed
H/h	Bring up the help screen
I	Increase image delay factor. Slows things down on very fast machines
L	Cancel the delay factor. Kaleidosonics will go as fast as it can
m	Advance to next mirror mode. The Kaleidosonics has four different mirror and reflection modes
M	Back up to the previous mirror mode
N/n	Advance to the next picture
P/p	Go to the previous picture
r	Increase screen roll
R	Decrease screen roll
S/s	Toggle digital sound effects on and off
T/t	Advance to the next texture map mode
U/u	Next/previous 3D shape
V/v	Increase/decrease volume of digital sound effects
W/w	Increase/decrease wave action in mirror modes 1 and 2
X/x	Cancel/increase x-axis rotation of 3D object
Y/y	Cancel/increase y-axis rotation of 3D object
Z/z	Cancel/increase z-axis rotation of 3D object
/	Toggle number of digital sound effects played simultaneously
F1-F4	Select number of simultaneous objects
F5	Turn mirror mode off

Key	Result
F6	Select reflection mirror mode
F7 - F10	Select spheres, circles, rings, or rings and spheres
+/-	Move horizon up/down, or increase/decrease brightness of image
[/]	Decrease/increase size of 3D object
0	Turn object display off
1-9	Set object movement speed
</>	Decrease/increase number of loops in circle
Spacebar	Toggle image recursion
Enter	Pressing once causes a zoom, twice zooms back to entire image
Arrows	Move lead object around the screen
Esc	Quit

Table 6-3 The effect of pressing different keys in Kaleidosonics

CHAPTER 7
General
Demonstrations

This final chapter describes a variety of material used for general presentations. From extensive interviews with the artists, you'll learn about the tricks and techniques used to make these demos really shine. For the most part, the work you will see is running under the control of Grasp, one of today's most powerful DOS-based multimedia authoring packages.

As you may recall from the section "How the MIDPAK/DIGPAK BigDemo Works" in Chapter 3, Grasp is a script-based system that offers superior flexibility and performance over icon-based packages. With it you can integrate flics, true-color images, MIDI music, and sound effects. Most importantly, Grasp can be expanded by way of add-in programs known as .GRPs. A great guide to learning Grasp is Philip Shaddock's *Multimedia Creations* from Waite Group Press (1992, ISBN 1-878139-26-3). Our focus in this chapter isn't to show you how to use Grasp, but rather to describe works created with it.

Ian Powelly's Animated Marketing has contributed six presentations to the collection, the majority of which are industrial simulations. You'll get an insight into how orthopedic surgery can be used to treat knee injuries from Dr. Randale Sechrest's Medical Multimedia Group. If you want to learn more about video modes and their impact on demo production, Karl Miller has described the various tradeoffs associated with different graphics resolutions. And on the lighter side, you'll be treated to some video footage in Tom Guthery's Mini Movie Theater. But the highlight of this chapter has to be the Waite Group Press Spring '94 catalog demo created by Philip Shaddock. It features an interactive journey through a huge space station modeled entirely in 3D Studio.

Karl Miller

Marketing Systems
Saskatoon, Saskatchewan, Canada
\DEMOS\MILLER
D-BRIDGE1   1.70MB
MARKSYS.EXE 1.9MB
REZDEMO   0.3MB

Figure 7-1 Harvey Crude from the
Marketing Systems demo

Marketing Systems is a management consulting practice specializing in marketing and communications planning. It is associated with PROFORM Development Corporation, a multimedia production company. Together they have developed and published computer software, institutional and promotional videos, animated computer simulations, computer screenshows, animated titles and logos, and interactive educational courseware. Their most recent accomplishment is a half-hour long corporate video produced entirely as PC animation. Using a combination of graphics, photos, and technical illustrations, a friendly cartoon oil drop by the name of Harvey Crude (see Figure 7-1) takes us inside his favorite refinery for an entertaining view of the transformation of raw stock into gasoline.

REZ-DEMO Demonstrates Different Graphics Modes

REZ-DEMO.EXE demonstrates the differences between file and screen resolutions. It presents the same image at 640x480 and 320x200, so it is particularly useful for educating clients about the tradeoffs between image quality and file size. The images were created with ComputerEyes Pro and are animated under the control of Grasp.

Producers and clients alike face a common dilemma when choosing the best resolution for a demonstration. Generally, choosing the number of colors to use is fairly simple. For the moment, 256 colors is usually the best choice. VGA is an almost universal PC video standard supporting up to 256 colors from a palette of 262,144 at 320x200 resolution. Naturally, 256-color displays at 640x480 produce even better images because more pixels mean sharper detail. Unfortunately, standard VGA supports only 16 colors at this resolution, but as SVGA systems supporting 640x480x256 colors rapidly replace VGA, more demo disks are being produced to run in SVGA mode. There are, however, significant limitations with SVGA as well.

All SVGA images and animations require considerably more disk space, run slower, need more memory, and take longer to create than their lower-resolution VGA equivalents. For example, the VGA photo in REZ-DEMO is a 33K .GIF file, while the SVGA one is 140K. If these files are then converted to the Grasp .PIC format used in these demos for faster loading, they grow at least twice as large. These issues may be minor if the production is always run on a dedicated computer, but they can be critical if the presentation must be distributed on floppy disk to multiple unknown systems.

The demo image shown in Figure 7-2 was taken from a 4 by 5 inch transparency using a Sony V101 Hi8 camcorder attached to a ComputerEyes Pro video digitizer. The resulting image was a 640x480x24-bit Targa file which was rescaled to 320x200 in Piclab, a shareware image processing program. Even though ComputerEyes is capable of capturing directly into 640x480x256 and 320x200x256 files, using Piclab for color reduction produces better results.

The last section of REZ-DEMO pans the 640x480 image across a 320x200 screen. Note how dramatically more efficient Grasp can be compared to other development tools. For example, the same pan effect created with Autodesk Animator's CONVERT utility would produce a 45-frame flic of 2.4MB. Grasp presents a smoother version of the same effect using a 48K image and two lines of code:

```
window 0 0 319 199      ;set window to full screen
fly 0 0 -86 -45 1 0 p1  ;"fly" the picture buffer across
```

Whenever considering display options, always run tests on the actual delivery system, especially if the production will be videotaped. Many people are surprised to learn that 320x200 mode often gives better results than higher resolutions when recorded on VHS. Because VHS is such a low-resolution format itself, the fine details in SVGA displays sometimes cause flicker, while VGA images are actually smoothed out and improved. Although higher-screen resolutions and greater color depth are becoming more common, 320x200x256 and 640x480x256 are still the best choices, particularly for displaying photographs.

This demo has provided Marketing Systems with a solid starting point from which to discuss the production and design issues of quality, production, presentation, file size, and cost with clients before actual work gets under way.

Figure 7-2 The 640x480 image from REZ-DEMO

D-BRIDG1.EXE Looping Demo for a Tradeshow

D-BRIDG1.EXE is a self-running screenshow produced for Develcon Electronics, an international manufacturer of communications hardware and software. This demo features their *bridge* products for internetwork communications links. Develcon exhibits at many trade shows around the world, so they approached Marketing Systems to create a a demo for use at these events. The promotional literature to be used as a starting point featured photos of the bridge products in front of futuristic backgrounds which, although attractive, bore no apparent relationship to the function of the five near-identical boxes that housed these bridge products. The challenge was graphically demonstrating differences between five products that look completely alike.

Marketing Systems designed this demo with the following objectives in mind:

 Provide a graphic representation of the firm's motto, "Behind every Develcon product is a lifetime warranty"

 Distinguish the purpose of each box

 Stress their Canadian origin

 Be able to run endlessly in a loop

 Compress the demo onto a single 5.25-inch floppy disk

To accomplish the first goal, the warranty crest was placed behind the corporate logo and behind each product. Karl developed animated symbols to reinforce each product's use, thus meeting the second goal. He used a flashing branch structure to associate with the three Ethernet bridges, and flashing loops for the two Token-Ring bridges. The third goal was not only to express national pride, but also to trade on the Canadian reputation for quality technology products. Attention was drawn to the Canadian red maple leaf by flying it across the screen and into place on the bridge product symbol.

The tight timeframe, potentially broad distribution, and need to fit the presentation onto one disk all mandated working in 320x200x256 colors. ComputerEyes Pro, CorelDraw, Autodesk Animator Pro, Piclab, Pictor, and Grasp from Paul Mace were the only tools used in the creation of this demo.

Some of the most challenging aspects of developing such a production are sometimes the least obvious. The corporate logo and warranty crest were supplied as 640x480 .CGM files. While the logo converted fairly well down to the 320x200 screen, the warranty crest required hours of retouching.

The task of zooming the crest from behind the logo, as shown in Figure 7-3, required many steps. Animator Pro was used to create the effect, but unfortunately images scaled by Animator Pro tend to be rather coarse. To create a smooth, solid look, Karl had to measure the crest in every Animator Pro frame, calculating its size as a percentage of the original and then using Piclab to rescale the original to the correct percentage before reloading these images back into Animator Pro.

The most interesting challenge was designing screens that would provide an attractive graphical layout for so many elements, particularly as the position of the product itself was

Figure 7-3 The zooming crest was stretched in 24-bit color using Piclab to assure maximum image quality

predetermined by the photo. There was also considerable logistical work developing palettes to accommodate both the photos and the animations and to manage the multiple layers as they were composited into the final product.

But by far the most entertaining part of the exercise was creating the tumbling leaf effect. To accomplish this, Karl made use of a feature of Animator Pro known as *optics*, which allows you to position a cel at a final destination while giving you complete control over the definition of the path it follows to arrive there.

The production got rave reviews. Trade show attendees often walk past a large number of audio-visual presentations, but most stopped to view this one. Its success can also be measured by the large number of Develcon dealers requesting copies for their own use. It seems they all liked the friendly little maple leaf that knew where it was going.

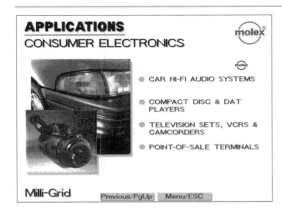

Charles Jameson

Silver Tongue Software
Wilmette, IL, USA
\DEMOS\JAMESON
MINIFIT.BAT　0.70MB
MOLEX.EXE　2.40MB

Figure 7-4 Choosing a 16-color palette composed of a range of varying intensities produces a good grayscale display for photographs

The two Grasp demos contributed by Silver Tongue Software were created for Molex Inc., a manufacturer of electrical connectors. Representatives of Molex regularly visit plants around the world giving these presentations on a variety of laptop computers. Having fully animated presentations gives Molex a distinct advantage in the often cramped and poorly lit cubicles of a corporate purchasing department. The Milligrid presentation provides an introduction to Molex as well as to their product line. The demo was designed with future expansion in mind; new products can easily be added to the main menu. The Minifit presentation was created later when salespeople realized that nothing conveyed the features of the products better than practical animations showing how they are used.

Chuck Jameson is a master at moving images between different color depths. If he is retouching photographs, he works in 24 bits so he has millions of colors available. For creating animations, Chuck runs Animator Pro, an 8-bit program, which limits him to a maximum of 256 colors. Finally, he reduces the images and animations down to 16 colors before integrating them into his distributable demo. He has no choice in this; the laptop computers meant to run these presentations are unable to display more than 16 colors.

Creating animations that work within this constraint of 16 levels of gray is always a challenge. In the case of these demos, Chuck chose a palette that provided variety not only in color but also in gray level. By assuring that no two colors in the palette would translate to approximately the same gray value, Chuck achieved a clear redisplay on the grayscale panel of the laptop.

However, to show photographs on a 16-color device requires a different set of rules. Generally, if you are looking for a common palette to use for a number of photographs, try one that consists of black, white, two grays, and three levels each of red, green, blue, and yellow. This type of static palette produces consistently good results. For an example check out the dithered photos of the applications in the Milligrid presentation (see Figure 7-4). While you can always get a better reduction to 16 colors by using a dithering algorithm that chooses the best 16 colors, the static-palette rule works best for most circumstances. Chuck points out that different products often give radically different results when reducing images down to 16 colors. His favorite is Photoshop, but he also uses Cricket Image, Graphics Workshop, and Piclab. (For another discussion of color reduction see the section "Great Color Reduction to the EGA Palette" in the first *Walkthroughs and Flybys CD*.

The product images used on the data sheet screens were based on the best pictures that the client had available. A great deal of time was spent converting grayscale scans, the output of a 3D modeling program, and orthographic drafting perspectives so that they all had the same look and feel.

The animation in the Minifit presentation could have been smoother except that the entire project had to fit on a single 720K diskette. While a smoother animation might have been more aesthetically pleasing, it would not have illustrated the products' features any better.

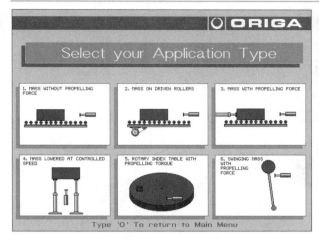

Ian Powelly

Animated Marketing Ltd.
Swindon, UK
\DEMOS\POWELLY

2500DEMO.EXE	1.44MBM
AVDEMO.EXE	1.3MB
IPDEMO.EXE	0.71MB
ORIGASAB.EXE	1.4MB
BIGMOL.EXE	1.23MB
PUMP.EXE	1.18MB
EMISSION.EXE	2.39MB

Figure 7-5 This demo runs a C program for floating-point calculations

Ian Powelly's Animated Marketing is one of the larger and more successful British presentation companies. While they do produce demo disks such as the one you will see for Dr. Solomon's Anti-virus Toolkit, their stock in trade is industrial simulations. All of the presentations in this section are Grasp demos.

Origa Shock Absorbers

Although the animation and graphics in this shock-absorber presentation are relatively simple (see Figure 7-5), the disk has proved highly effective as a sales and training aid. The need to fit the presentation onto a single disk restricted the use of conventional animation to an absolute minimum. Instead heavy use was made of color cycling and palette changes to achieve many of the animation effects.

Because Grasp doesn't handle floating-point math, Ian wrote a program in C to determine the correct shock absorber for a particular use. As you can see, the integration of this external C program is completely transparent to the user.

Belliss & Morcom Compressor

The moving parts of the compressor presentation (see Figure 7-6) are achieved by playing a flic, while the red flowing effect is created by manipulating the palette. Even though every frame in a flic file contains its own palette assignment information, Grasp has a feature that allows you to override this setting and alter the palette programmatically. Using this technique, you can create a nice flowing effect just by rotating palette indices without having to change the underlying pattern at all. In other words, suppose the red flowing bits of the flic used here are contained in palette indices 1 through 5. When the second frame of the flic

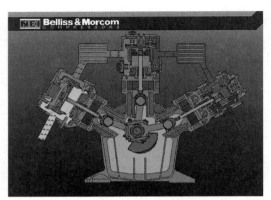

Figure 7-6 This animation of a pump makes use of palette cycling while playing a standard flic file

comes to the screen, each of these values is shifted along one position so that the value of palette index 1 becomes the color that was in index 2. Index 2 gets the color that was in index 3, and so on. This is a cool trick; to create the same effect using Animator Pro's palette-handling would have resulted in a much larger file.

Despite its imperfections, this demo has proved to have countless uses over the two years since it was completed. Mainly, it is used as an attraction running on a large screen at trade shows, but it has also been valuable in explaining the potential of standard SVGA graphics for demonstrating complex technical and industrial products.

Dr. Solomon's Anti-Virus Toolkit

This demo for a software product has a great opening, using a tabloid-style shock tactic to get the user's attention. It then goes on to demonstrate how relatively simple dynamic graphics can convey a complex message in a concise and entertaining way. The casual graphic style, shown in Figure 7-7, was deliberately chosen to counterbalance the highy technical content. The entertaining delivery and effective use of graphics has opened the eyes of a number of direct-mail agencies to the creative potential of the demo disk.

A wide range of graphical and programming techniques were implemented in Grasp to create this demo, such as bitmap animation, double-buffered graphics, code-generated images, random number generation, palette fades, and some quite complex animation algorithms for the virus simulations. Because the presentation had to run from a floppy disk, .GIF files were used to hold all of the images.

Ian points out that thousands of products and companies can benefit from the use of this relatively basic level of multimedia. This represents a huge potential market for graphics developers who have the right engineering background, particularly as more and more sales forces become equipped with color notebook PCs for administration and presentation purposes.

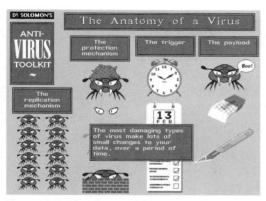

Figure 7-7 Simple graphics are used to convey a complicated topic

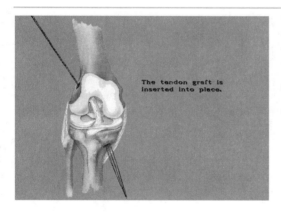

Dr. Randale Sechrest

Medical Multimedia Group
Libby, MT, USA
\DEMOS\SECHREST

MMGDEMO.BAT	0.66MB
KNEE.BAT	0.59MB
TREAT.BAT	2.59MB

Figure 7-8 These animations are used in a clinical setting

Medical Multimedia Group focuses on the development of medical software for general distribution, but also takes on custom projects. Randale has sent in three interactive demonstrations of patient education programs used in a clinical setting.

The complex procedures involved in orthopedic surgery can be difficult to explain. The use of animation simplifies this by giving the doctor and patient a common point of reference. Figure 7-8 shows a screen from the presentation for those suffering from knee injuries. Randale feels that the health industry is just beginning to use computers to interact with patients in a meaningful way and looks forward to exciting times ahead. (For more information on work done by this group see the section "A Medical Application to Inform and Document Patient Consent" in the first *Walkthroughs and Flybys CD*.)

Philip Shaddock

Shaddock Multimedia Design
Vancouver, BC, Canada
\DEMOS\SHADDOCK
NANO.EXE   1.85MB
CATALOG.BAT 69.40MB

Figure 7-9 A scene from the Waite
Group Press Spring '94 catalog

Both of the demos that follow were created by Grasp guru and fellow Waite Group Press author Philip Shaddock. Philip has written them both to take advantage of a Sound Blaster, provided that you first load the FM driver file SBFMDRV.COM. If you are running this demo through the main menu user interface, it will take care of that for you.

WGP Spring '94 Catalog

The Spring '94 catalog is probably one of the more ambitious demonstrations ever created for free distribution. There is no storyline or suggested running order, which means the user can wander at random through the halls and rooms of this virtual academy. To help you find your way, an animating "gobot" takes over your mouse cursor. When the gobot points to the left, right, or ahead, you are free to move in one of those directions. A wagging finger means that access is not allowed.

The Waite Group Academy is circular in layout, with six rooms around the perimeter and a large central hub. Corridors allow access between each of the rooms and the hub. All of the new books for the spring season are in one room, while Waite Group's first software product, VR Basic, is in another. There is a ship's gallery where you can view still images, as well as a backlist room where you can access a database of all the Waite Group Press titles. Should you want to order a book, you can print out an order form that is convenient to fax. One of the most amazing sequences is the finale when you depart the Academy from the observation deck, shown in Figure 7-9.

The overall concept and general specification for this demo came from Mitchell Waite. Philip Shaddock did all of the production and planning, and most of the programming. Mike Miller created all of the 3D animations in Autodesk 3D Studio. Some of the trickier menu code and printing routines were written by Don Magnusson.

The Nanotechnology Demo

The Nanotechnology demo accompanies *Nanotechnology Playhouse* by Christopher Lampton, Waite Group Press, 1993. Nanotechnology, an unusual branch of science, postulates that someday machines will be designed and constructed at the atomic level. The goal of both the book and the demo is to shrink your perspective to such a degree that you can conceptualize just how small these machines would be.

Tom Guthery

FLIX Productions
DelValle, TX, USA
\DEMOS\GUTHERY
FLIXDEMO.EXE   2.04MB

Figure 7-10 The Mini Movie Theater plays over 50 video clips, yet is small enough to be compressed onto a single diskette

As a hobby, Tom creates animated graphics software for children. The first *Walkthroughs and Flybys CD* included a copy of his Animated Words program that helps kids practice the most basic of reading skills. For more background information on Tom, see his section in Chapter 4.

For this book, Tom supplied the Mini Movie Theater, a screen from which is shown in Figure 7-10. While this demo has no game element, you can choose to replay the current video clip by pressing the Play button or advance to the next clip by selecting the Next button. Use the (←) and (→) keys to highlight your menu choice and then press the (ENTER) key to trigger your selection. As there are over 40 different sections to this little demo, only the highlights are pointed out in Table 7-1. Keep in mind that all of the animations share the same palette, which accounts for the relatively poor image quality.

Demo Number	Contents
1	Time lapse of a banana being peeled and eaten
7	An indian paintbrush (native flower) staged on a rotating coaster against a black velvet background
16	This reverse time-lapse of melting ice cream took about an hour. The frames were grabbed by the computer unattended
18	An exploding pencil created with progressively stronger applications of Animator Pro's Jumble ink
22	This animation of a piece of clay has been reversed as the model was destroyed during the filming
28	Cigarette smoke was captured in full motion before being reversed and smoothed
42	The extreme bottom of the dancing tools are not shown so as to hide the stiff wire holding them to wooden stands. When the wire became visible, it was painted out

Table 7-1 Highlights of the first section of Mini Movie Theater

The second section shifts into 640x480x16 color mode. For the Animated Money sequence, two gradations each of eight colors were assigned for the silver and the copper. As there are no other hues in the scene, the result is a beautifully realistic image. The morphing was created with the Gryphon Morph program.

Following the morphing coins is an interesting sequence of a hummingbird. The original file was over 3MB in size, but by setting the Microsoft Video 1 compression algorithm to use a very high setting, everything in the scene becomes unrecognizable except for the moving parts of the bird. The end result is almost a watercolor effect.

One of the last animations in the demo, of a lightbulb and hammer, was created using some special tricks. The lightbulb is actually a balloon that is progressively deflated. The hammer was digitized separately, and the elements were composited together with Animator Pro. The explosion was created by applying stronger and stronger Jumble ink to move the pixels farther and farther from their source positions over multiple frames.

Stephen Steininger

Quantum Technologies
Granger IN, USA
Q_PIPE.EXE   2.13MB
Q_LINK.EXE   1.92MB

Q_LINK.EXE is a 180-frame repeating animation running at 640x480x256 colors. The idea originated from a piece of chain Stephen found in his basement. In thinking about what the inventor of this type of chain must have gone through, this particular form sprang to mind.

The Q_LINK animation was modelled in MacroModel V1.5 on the PC and a Renderman .RIB file was exported for every two degrees of rotation. Renderman was then used to create a series of .TGA, files which were consolidated into a common palette with TGAPIC before the discreet frames were assembled into an animation with Grasp's GDFF program. The Q_PIPE animation found in the same directory was created using a similiar approach.

Contributor Listings

This appendix provides a list of all the artists who contributed animations, demos, or programs to this book. The list is in alphabetical order by last name, since many of these artists are hobbyists working for no particular company. All of the phone numbers listed are in the form one would dial from within that country. The name of each artist's best piece is included as the last line in their listing. All addresses are in the USA unless otherwise noted.

Jeff Alu
2535 Chestnut Ave.
Orange, CA 92667
Tel: 714-633-8051
Email:70733.1445@compuserve.com
OFFANI.FLI

Juan Carlos Arevalo
Apdo. Correos 156405
28080-Madrid
Spain
Tel: 34-1-415-8499
INCONEXI

David Bleecker
Dept. of Mathematics
University of Hawaii
Honolulu, HI 96822
Tel: 808-956-4670
GLASS.FLC

Niko Boese
Troubadix Studio
Rotdornallee 16
2000 Hamburg 71
Germany
Tel: 49-06414946
.VOC format sound bites

Simon Browne
Parallel Universe
310 Brown Hill Road
London SE6 1AX
UK
Tel: 081-461-4233
Email:100410.534@compuserve.com
The SpaceBar

John Byrnes
1016 Grove St.
Maitland, FL 32751
Tel: 407-629-1199
DRAGON.FLI

Florentin Cristian
5102 Panama Ave.
Richmond, CA 94804
Tel: 510-526-0240
FLIGHTX2.FLI

Adrian Dodds Design
9 Eden Way
Bicester, Oxfordshire OX6 8RP
UK
Tel: 0869-246928
CULINAIR.FLC

Merlin Farmer
Crystal Cave Computers
103 Barr Street
Cartersville, IL 62918
Tel: 619-985-8154
Email:74650.1164@compuserve.com
DIAMONDS.FLI

Jason Gibbs
Interactive Media Solutions
4 High Street
Twyford, Berks RG10 9AE
UK
Tel: 0734-344666
Email: 100030.53@compuserve.com
Grasp drivers for The BigDemo

Tom Guthery IV
FLIX Productions
Rt. 1 Box 601
DelValle, TX 78617
Tel:512-247-3974
Email:72740.1326@compuserve.com
STARSHIP.FLI

Thomas Hellesen
DarkZone
Belsetsvingen 16.
1349 Rykkinn
Norway
Tel: 67130296
Debut

Ulrik Henriksen
Surprise!Productions
Stensagervej 5A ST
8260 Viby J
Denmark
Tel: 86119444
Email: v12@dec5102.aarhues.dk
The Good, the Bad, and the Ugly

Charles Jameson
Silver Tongue Software
343 Central Ave.
Wilmette, IL 60091-1941
Tel: 708-256-3122
Email:71350.1014@compuserve.com
Molex

Chris Johnston
NASA Lewis Research Center
21000 Brookpark Rd.
MS105-1
Cleveland, OH 44135
Email: chris@szvzh.lerc.nasa.gov
PMZ.FLC

Sami Kapanen
Epical
Naakantie 10
13500 HML
Finland
Tel: 358-17-6380820
BBS: 358-17-6184040
Takeover

Richard Lapidus
Video Production Marketing
4840 NW 28th Ave.
Boca Raton, FL 33434
Tel: 407-241-2961
Email: 71172.1451@compuserve.com
The Basketball

Timo Ludwig
Xography
Scheurebenweg 14
55278 Mommenheim
Germany
Email: FIDO: 2:247/169
Elements

Pero Maticevic
MWM Design
144 Elgin Ave.
London.W9 2NT
UK
The Blade water sculpture

John McIvor
27778 Gamble Bay Rd. NE
Kingston, WA 98346
Tel: 206-634-2540, ext. 8038
MELONFRM.FLI

John McManus
38 Fentiman Ave.
Ottawa, K1S 0T6
Canada
Tel: 613-993-9305
STARSTUF.FLC

Bruce Meikle
Fire Media
507 King St. E, Suite 16
Toronto, Ontario, M5A 1M3
Canada
Email:72614.2334@compuserve.com
RADARSAT.FLI

Karl Miller
Marketing Systems
P.O. Box 9151
Saskatoon, SK S7K 7E8
Canada
Email: 73720.2100@compuserve.com
REZDEMO

Michael Mulholland
97 Devonshire Road
Birmingham B20 2PG
UK
Tel: 021-523-4464
Email: 76370.3220@compuserve.com
Killer Chess II

Grahame Naylor
Magic Lantern Ltd.
Metropolitan Wharf
London E1 9SS
UK
Tel: 071-480-6811
Email:100013.1340@compuserve.com
OFFICE.FLI

Ingo Neuman
Karl-Glassing-Strasse 5
65183 Wiesbaden
Germany
Email: 100136.155@compuserve.com
Wooden man

Perttu Poikonen
Epical
Honkolantie 74
44160 Huutomaki
Finland
Takeover

Erik Pojar
Surprise!Productions
Siegfriedstrasse 55
1210 Vienna
Austria
Tel: 43-12154457
Email: smarton@email.tuwien.ac.at
The Good, the Bad, and the Ugly

Ian Powelly
Animated Marketing
34 Broughton Grange
Swindon, Wiltshire SN3 1LW
UK
Email: 100063.20@compuserve.com
Dr. Solomon's demo

John W. Ratcliff
The Audio Solution
747 Napa Lane
St. Charles, MO 63304
Email: 70253.3237@compuserve.com
BBS: 314-939-0200
MIDPAK and DIGPAK

Thomas Reimann
Im Haufland 20
8627 Grueningen
Switzerland
Tel: 41-1-9353692
Email: 70134.2657@compuserve.com
CRAB7CD.FLI

Dan Richardson
109 Laurel Park
Northhampton. MA 01060
Tel: 413-684-7351
Email: 72537.1341@compuserve.com
BUCKA640.FLC

Jeff Rouyer
3212 Lake Park Way, #304
Longmont, CO 80503
Tel: 303-678-9558
Email: jrouyer@aol.com
WHIRLI.FLI

Paul Russam
The Electric Drawing Board
35-37 Alfred Place
London WC1 7DP
UK
Tel: 071-580-7302
Chernobyl encasement

Randale Sechrest
Medical Multimedia Group
308 Lousiana Ave.
Libby, MT 59923
Tel: 406-293-9350
Email: 71131.602@compuserve.com
Knee injuries

Philip Shaddock
2715 W. 2nd Ave.
Vancouver, BC V6K 1K2
Canada
Tel: 604-732-9917
Email: 70274.2146@compuserve.com
Waite Group Catalog

Phil Shatz
Media Development Services
Vigilant House
120 Wilton Road
London, SW1V 1JZ
UK
Tel: 071-233-9924
Fax: 071-931-8041
Email: 76470.233@compuserve.com

Robert Stein III
Anigraf/x
P.O. Box 1715
Jacksonville, OR 97530
Tel: 503-772-6525
3D Studio Release 3 image

Stephen Steininger
Quantum Technologies
12126 Timberline Trace
Granger, IN 46530-9137
Q_LINK.EXE

Erik Stridell
Cascada
Rotevagen 1
S-735 33 Surahammar
Sweden
Tel: 46 22033489
Hex Appeal

Samuli Syvahuoko
Future Crew
Hiiralantie 27a
02160 Espoo
Finland
Email: jtheinon@cc.helsinki.fi
Second Reality

Rob Wallace
Wallace Music & Sound Inc.
P.O. Box 393
13636 North 59th Ave.
Glendale, AZ 85304
Tel: 602-979-6201
Email: 29220@ef.gc.maricopa.edu
or 71042.1410@compuserve.com
Multimedia Kaleidosonics

Chris Young
3119 Cossell Drive
Indianapolis, IN 46224
Email: 76702.1655@compuserve.com
Hexpanding Universe

Troubleshooting

The next several pages try to anticipate the problems some users may face. If this section proves inadequate in the resolution of your problem, send me email at 76470.233@compuserve.com. Many problems that you may encounter are related to memory configuration. For more detailed information on memory problems, we recommend *Memory Management in a Multimedia World* (Waite Group Press, 1994); or see your DOS documentation.

Problem with ANIPLAY Configuration

Problem   **When I open the Screen Size dialog box to set a 640x480 resolution driver, there is no option available for that screen size.**

Solution   You don't have a VESA driver installed. First, check the book and disks that came with your PC or graphics card for a reference to a VESA driver and follow the directions for its installation. If you can't find one, then you should download a copy of Stefan Harmann's Universal VESA Driver, which you can find in the CompuServe ASOFT forum. At present the file is named UVESA3.ZIP and it's located in library nine. You could also look it up under Stefan's userid number, 72017,3216.

Problem with Sound Card Configuration

Problem   **The program asks if music is playing ok, but I can't hear anything.**

Solution   If you don't hear any music during the configuration process and one of these programs thinks it's playing audio, there is a chance that your volume levels are set too low. On the Sound Blaster 16, you would use the SB16SET program to check the volume levels.

The DMP BigDemo Won't Run

If you are having trouble running the DMP BigDemo, chances are the cause of your problem is that you either don't have EMS (expanded memory) available or that your BLASTER environment variable is set incorrectly. For instructions on how to edit your CONFIG.SYS file to activate EMS memory, see the section *Read This Before Using the CD* at the beginning of this book. For further information on the BLASTER environment variable, see your sound card documentation.

Problem **Artist title screens are shown continuously one after another, but there is no sound. The only way out of the infinite loop is to reboot.**

Solution You are using a Sound Blaster and have an incorrect BLASTER environment setting. This could be caused by removing your Sound Blaster 16 from the machine and then replacing it without running SBCONFIG. Run SBCONFIG so that the BLASTER string is recreated. If you are using a Sound Blaster clone, run your sound card's diagnostics software and check that a BLASTER environment string does exist.

Problem **The artist title screens are shown continuously but the words "Memory Manager Error" also come up. There is no sound and you need to reboot.**

Solution You need to have expanded memory for the DMP music player to work and still leave enough free RAM for the flic player and the program to fade down the music. Check your CONFIG.SYS file for a NOEMS switch on the DEVICE=EMM386 line and replace NOEMS with RAM. If you are running DOS 6 or higher, try running MEMMAKER if the problem persists.

Problem **After the medley of animations at the start of the DMP BigDemo, the words "Memory Manager Error" flash up briefly on screen before the next sequence of music and animation starts. The same thing happens when you try to press (ENTER) to go to next sequence or if you press (ESC) to terminate.**

Solution You need to have expanded memory for the DMP music player to work and still leave enough free RAM for the flic player and the program to fade down the music. Check your CONFIG.SYS file for a NOEMS switch on the DEVICE=EMM386 line and replace NOEMS with RAM. If you are running DOS 6 or higher, try running MEMMAKER if the problem persists.

Problem **I get the error message "There is no BLASTER environment variable pointing to the Sound Blaster card!"**

Solution If your sound card is a Sound Blaster from Creative Labs, you have not properly installed it, so some system configuration information is missing from the DOS environment. Sound Blaster clone owners have not configured their systems to run in Sound Blaster compatibility mode.

Problem   **I get the error message "BLASTER environment variable is incorrect because there is no Sound Blaster at I/0: 220, DMA:1, IRQ: 5!"**

Solution   The values in the error message for I/O, DMA, and IRQ may be different in your case, but if you get this information, your sound card is almost certainly configured incorrectly. If you have a Sound Blaster 16 and you have forced a non-default IRQ setting through the SBCONFIG program and then removed and replaced the Sound Blaster, you will get this message because the values in the EPROM on the card have been lost. If you ever remove and replace your sound card, it is a good idea to reinstall the software.

Problem   **Music plays, but PC locks up, requiring a power-down to reset the system.**

Solution   Grasp is unable to close the DMA channel through which it is talking to your sound card. This error may occur on Sound Blaster clone cards that just aren't close enough to the Creative Labs standard. There is no resolution to this problem other than replacing your sound card.

The MIDPAK BigDemo Crashes

Problem   **I get the error message "Memory Manager Error - Not enough memory to allocate block."**

Solution   You need to have at least 520K of free conventional memory in order to run The BigDemo. If you are running DOS 5.0 or later, check the amount of memory you have free by entering **MEM** at the DOS command line. The most important number here is next to the line at the bottom of the listing that reads *Largest Executable Program Size*. If that number is less than 520,000, you have to change your system configuration to run The BigDemo.

   The first thing to try is commenting out any TSR programs or device drivers that you won't need while using *Modeling the Dream CD*. Network drivers, in particular, occupy large amounts of RAM, so commenting those out should be your highest priority. If you are running DOS version 6.0 or later, try running MEMMAKER to optimize your system configuration. If you are still stuck, you may wish to try a memory-management utility program like QEMM from Quarterdeck.

Sources

This appendix contains a list of products from companies that have been mentioned in the text. The major section comprises a list of all the books that were used as sources by the contributors and authors. The other sections list all other products.

Books

Modeling the Dream CD is a sequel to *Walkthroughs and Flybys CD*, by Phil Shatz, Waite Group Press, 1993, ISBN 1-878739-40-9.

The Future Crew recommends the following books as the reference materials they use to create demos such as Second Reality:

Mastering Turbo Assembler, Tom Swan, Hayden Books 1989,
　　ISBN 0-672-48435-8
PC System Programming, Michael Tischer, Abacus 1990, ISBN 1-55755-036-0
The Programmers PC Sourcebook, Thom Hogan, Microsoft Press 1988,
　　ISBN 1-55615-118-7
Programming the 80386, J. Crawford and P. Gelsinger, Sybex 1987,
　　ISBN 0-89588-381-3
Programmers Guide to EGA and VGA, R. Ferraro, Addison Wesley 1989,
　　ISBN 0-201-12692-3

If you are interested in creating fractals such as the nebula seen out of the window of The SpaceBar, Simon Browne recommends the following two books:

Fractal Creations 2E, Wegner and Tyler, Waite Group Press, 1994,
ISBN 1-878739-34-4
Fractals for Windows, Wegner, et al, Waite Group Press, 1994,
ISBN 1-878739-25-5

Image Lab is a fantastic guide to using the Piclab image processing utility. A number of other interesting programs for drawing and converting between formats are also included.

Image Lab, Tim Wegner, Waite Group Press, 1993,
ISBN 1-878739-11-5

Ray-tracing with POV-Ray and Polyray are the subjects of the following books:

Animation How-To CD, Jeff Bowermaster, Waite Group Press, 1993,
ISBN 1-878739-54-9
Ray Tracing Creations, Chris Young and Drew Wells, Waite Group Press, 1993,
ISBN 1-878739-27-1
Making Movies on Your PC, David K. Mason and Alexander Enzmann,
Waite Group Press, 1993, ISBN 1-878739-41-1

If you want to learn Grasp, the book to get is:

Multimedia Creations, Philip Shaddock, Waite Group Press, 1992,
ISBN 1-878739-26-3

For information about music and sound effects, see these two books:

Music and New Technology MIDI Companion, Jacobs and Georghiades, Sigma, 1992,
ISBN: 1-850582-31-9
Sound Effects Playhouse, Kevin Weiner, Waite Group Press, 1993,
ISBN 1-878739-36-0

For an overview of CD-ROM technology in a book packed with useful information get:

Publish Yourself on CD-ROM, Caffarelli and Straughan, Random House, 1992,
ISBN 0-679-74297-2

If you are interested in real-time rendering on the PC, the following book will be of interest:

Virtual Reality Creations, Stampe, Roehl and Eagan, Waite Group Press, 1993,
ISBN 1-878739-39-5

Software

Addresses for the following companies should be assumed to be located in the USA unless otherwise noted.

ARJ

Robert K. Jung
2606 Village Road West
Norwood, MA 02062
Email: robjung@world.std.com

ARJ is the compression standard used to store certain files on the *Modeling the Dream* disc.

Autodesk 3D Studio, Autodesk Animator Pro

Autodesk Inc.
2320 Marinship Way
Sausalito, CA 94965
Tel: 415-332-2344
Fax: 415-331-8093
CompuServe: GO ASOFT

3D Studio is the "Black and Decker" of virtual reality creation. Animator Pro is the companion editing program. If you are interested in Autodesk multimedia products, an excellent resource is the *Autodesk Multimedia Resource Guide* which you can get by calling 800-879-4233.

BATCOM

Wenham Software Co.
5 Burley Street
Wenham, MA 01984
Tel: 508-774-7036

This batch file compiler proved to be indispensible in the course of this project. It was used to create the installation program for *Modeling the Dream CD*.

Deluxe Paint IIE and Deluxe Paint Animation

Electronic Arts
1450 Fashion Island Blvd.
San Mateo, CA 94404
Tel: 415-571-7171
Fax: 415-570-5137

Leaders in the production of home entertainment software for the PC, this company also publishes the two popular Deluxe Paint drawing programs.

DMP-Dual Mod Player

Otto Chrons
Vaajakatu 5 K 199
Fin-33720 Tampere
Finland
Email:Otto.Chrons@cc.tut.fi

Gryphon Morph

Gryphon Software Corporation
7220 Trade Street #120
San Diego, CA 92121-2325
Tel: 619-536-8815
Fax: 619-536-8932
Email: gryphonsw@aol.com

Grasp

Paul Mace Software
400 Williamson Way
Ashland, OR 97520
Tel: 503-488-0224
Fax: 503-488-1549
BBS: 503-482 7435
Email: CompuServe: GO GRASP

Many of the demos on *Modeling the Dream CD* have been produced with Grasp. The acronym, *GRaphic Animation System for Professionals,* says it all.

Macromodel

Macromedia
600 Townsend St.
San Francisco, CA 941103
Tel: 415-252-2000

Macromodel is the Windows-based modeling package contributor Steve Steininger uses to write out Renderman .RIB files.

MIDPAK/DIGPAK

John W. Ratcliff at The Audio Solution
747 Napa Lane
St. Charles, MO 63304
Email: 70253.3237@compuserve.com
BBS: 314-939-0200

For more information about integrating MIDPAK and DIGPAK into your own applications, contact John Ratcliff at The Audio Solution.

Multimedia Kaleidosonics

Masque Publishing
P.O. Box 5223
Englewood, CO 80155
Tel: 303-290-9853
Fax: 303-290-6303

Kaleidosonics is an interactive kaleidoscope programmed by John Ratcliff with excellent music accompaniment by Rob Wallace.

Sound Forge

Monty Schmidt at Sonic Foundry
100 South Baldwin, Suite 204
Madison, WI 53703
Tel: 608-256-5555
Email: 73020.2770@compuserve.com

Sound Forge is Rob Wallace's wave-form editing program of choice.

Virtual Reality Toolkit

DoMark Inc
1900 South Norfolk St. #202
San Mateo, CA 94403
Tel: 415-513-8929
Fax:415-571-0437

DoMark Software Ltd.
51-57 Lacy Road
Putney, London SW15 1PR. UK
Tel: 081-780-2222

The Virtual Reality Toolkit is a low-cost package that creates 3D worlds through which the user can move interactively with a mouse. In the UK, it is sold under the name of the DoMark 3D Construction Kit.

WinOnCD

CeQuadrat
Dennewartstraße 27
5100 Aachen
Germany
Tel: 0241-9631100
Fax: 0241-9631101

WinOnCD is the finest program currently available for premastering CD-ROMs on the Philips CDD531 desktop recorder.

PC Audio Cards

The Sound Blaster AWE

Creative Labs, Inc.
1901 McCarthy Blvd.
Milpitas, CA 95035
Tel: 408-428-6600
Fax: 408-428-6611
Email: 72662.1602@compuserve.com
UK-based BBS: ++44(0)743-360287
CompuServe: GO BLASTER

The Sound Blaster AWE is one of the best all-around PC-based audio cards available. It combines a wealth of features with an affordable price tag.

The Gravis UltraSound

Advanced Gravis Computer Technology Ltd
101-3750 North Fraser Way
Burnaby, BC, V5J 5E9
Canada
Tel: 604-431-1807
Fax: 604-451-9358
BBS: 604-451-5927
Email: john.smith@gravis.com

The Gravis UltraSound is favored by demo developers in The Scene because of its ability to produce sound quality superior to the Sound Blaster while using radically fewer CPU cycles.

Standards and Specifications

International MIDI Association
23634 Emelita St.
Woodland Hills, CA 91367
Tel: 818-598-0088

A printed copy of the Standard MIDI Specification costs $11.50 at this time, and can be obtained by writing the association.

Video Electronics Standards Association (VESA)
1330 South Bascom Avenue, Suite D
San Jose, CA 95128-4502

VESA publishes standards governing various aspects of PC graphics compatibility.

INDEX

Books have a substantial influence on the destruction of the forests of the Earth. For example, it takes 17 trees to produce one ton of paper. A first printing of 30,000 copies of a typical 480-page book consumes 108,000 pounds of paper which will require 918 trees!

Waite Group Press™ is against the clear-cutting of forests and supports reforestation of the Pacific Northwest of the United States and Canada, where most of this paper comes from. As a publisher with several hundred thousand books sold each year, we feel an obligation to give back to the planet. We will therefore support and contribute a percentage of our proceeds to organizations which seek to preserve the forests of planet Earth.

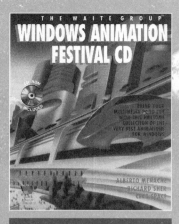

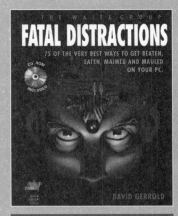
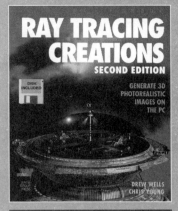

SATISFACTION REPORT CARD

Please fill out this card if you wish to know of future updates to
Modeling the Dream CD or to receive our catalog.

Company Name: _____

Division/Department: _____   Mail Stop: _____

Last Name: _____   First Name: _____   Middle Initial: _____

Street Address: _____

City: _____   State: _____   Zip: _____

Daytime telephone: (   ) _____

Date product was acquired: Month _____   Day _____   Year _____   Your Occupation: _____

Overall, how would you rate *Modeling the Dream CD*?
☐ Excellent   ☐ Very Good   ☐ Good
☐ Fair   ☐ Below Average   ☐ Poor

What did you like MOST about this product? _____
_____

What did you like LEAST about this product? _____
_____

How do you use this book (education, diversion, relaxation...)?
_____

Please describe any problems you may have encountered with
Modeling the Dream CD? _____
_____

What is your level of computer expertise?
☐ New   ☐ Dabbler   ☐ Hacker
☐ Power User   ☐ Programmer   ☐ Experienced Professional

What computer languages are you familiar with? _____
_____
_____

Please describe your computer hardware:
Computer _____   Hard disk _____
5.25" disk drives _____   3.5" disk drives _____
Video card _____   Monitor _____
Printer _____   Peripherals _____
Sound board _____   CD ROM _____

Where did you buy this book?
☐ Bookstore name:
☐ Discount store name:
☐ Computer store name:
☐ Catalog name:
☐ Direct from WGP
☐ Other _____

What price did you pay for this book? _____

What influenced your purchase of this book?
☐ Recommendation   ☐ Advertisement
☐ Magazine review   ☐ Store display
☐ Mailing   ☐ Book's format
☐ Reputation of The Waite Group   ☐ Topic

How many computer books do you buy each year? _____
How many other Waite Group books do you own? _____
What is your favorite Waite Group book? _____
_____

Additional comments? _____
_____
_____

Send to: Waite Group Press, Inc.
                  Attn: *Modeling the Dream CD*
                  200 Tamal Plaza
                  Corte Madera, CA 94925

☐ Check here for a free Waite Group catalog

Modeling the Dream CD